Contemporary
Knitting
by Jo Sharp

Contemporary Knitting

Editor Jo Sharp

Design & Pattern Writing
Jo Sharp, Leanne Prouse, Fiona Ramsay,
Wendy Richards, Rachelle King

Sub-Editor Megan Fisher

Knitting Our dedicated team of hand knitters

Graphic Design Becky Chilcott, Chil3

Layouts & Typesetting Bronia Richards

Photography
Robert Frith, Acorn Photo Agency

Styling Bronia Richards, Fiona Ramsay

Hair & Makeup Suzanne Lane

Associate Publisher Mary-Elaine Tynan

CEO / Publisher	Prema Perera
Director Business Development	Janice Williams
Sales Director	Denis Ford
Sales Development Manager	Karl Hayes
Finance & Administration Manager	Vicky Mahadeva
Circulation Manager	Shayne McNally
Creative Director	Dave Mann
Editorial Production Manager	Kerry Boyne
Print Production Manager	Renata Alvarez
Advertising Production Manager	Margaret Swerdlow

Circulation enquiries to our Sydney head office (02) 9805 0399.
Contemporary Knitting No. 2 is published by Universal Magazines, Unit 5, 6-8
Byfield Street, North Ryde 2113. Phone: (02) 9805 0399, Fax: (02) 9805 0714.
Melbourne office, 16 Princess Street, Kew 3101 (03) 9853 1346, Fax: (03) 9853
5929. Printed by Times Printers Pte Ltd, Singapore. Distributed by Newsagent
Direct Distribution, 9353 9911. NZ Distributor: Tiffanies Treasures Ph (09) 473
6275, fax (09) 473 6274. Uk Distributor: Auscraft Publications Ltd, Ph +44 1488
649 955, fax +44 1488 649 950. US Distributor: Stonehouse Publications,
Ph 1800 461 1640.

* Recommended retail price
ISSN 1149-5643
Copyright Universal Magazines MMV
ACN 003 026 944
www.universalshop.com

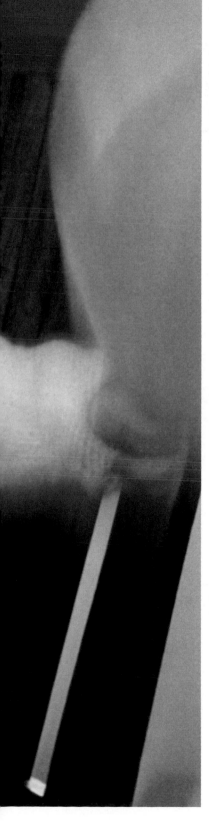

contents

a word from the editor

Bless your cotton socks!

This soft & luscious issue of Contemporary Knitting extends its horizons and gives readers more to get their needles into. We've been investigating the rapidly rising neo-knitting phenomena and exploring the reasons, habits and preferences of today's knitters. We hope you'll enjoy our feature interview with a dynamic young professional woman who knits for pleasure. She lives near the city where she works as an accountant during the day, teaches accountancy at night and dances in her spare time. Her story will re-ignite the flame of creativity in the context of contemporary lives. Find out more on page 10.

In this issue we are officially in arty party mode and expanding into pastel shades and edible textures. We've made bundles of enticing cushions to give your space a look of luxury while you're relaxing or entertaining family and friends.

And stepping slightly left of knitting, we have a story about the ancient craft of Japanese Katazome stencil printing. Our guest writer, Sue Leighton-White, explores the origins of the antique fabrics featured and shares a pattern for a knitting carry bag made from a quilted Japanese print fabric.

Because we know it's very common for knitters to be working on a number of projects at the same time, we've included lots of small portable items in this issue, knitting that is easily taken up and put aside. As always you will find plenty of knitting for beginners along with a few challenging projects for those who are further along in their knitting skills.

Enjoying the ritual of giving and receiving is very much about being at home. We really have had so much fun wrapping pressies and finding children to invite to a "party" for our photos. And when all the gifting and giggling is done, it's so great to relax with loved ones and enjoy being surrounded by soft surfaces, wearing a gift from a favourite friend, some cuddly knitted cotton socks...

Enjoy!

Jo Sharp

"It's become my retreat, a way to turn my thoughts away from work at the end of the day."

knitting
connections

Knitter Profile

Kristy Holloway

Knitting has been the glue for keeping generations of family and friends together.

Choosing a place to knit is all about having enough elbow room for twenty six year old accountant, Kristy Holloway.

At home on the couch she must have the end of the chair to herself, because she can't knit when she's elbowing the person next to her. But otherwise, this very passionate and engaging young woman fits knitting in between her work as a chartered accountant, ballet instructor and evening book-keeping tutor.

Her current swag of projects includes cushions, throws and homewares, which are all part of the preparation for her move to a newly renovated apartment in a riverside suburb near Perth in Western Australia. With an eye for colour and detail, her knitting is particularly inspiring. Huge Intarsia floor cushions, a soft "woven stitch" throw, a cabled throw and knitted cushions, delicately embroidered and all beautifully colour coordinated in rich romantic shades.

Kristy's Nanna, Peggy, first taught her to knit during holidays when she was in primary school.

Kristy explained, "usually by the next holidays I had forgotten again, but Nanna persevered with me and eventually it stuck. She recently taught me cable knitting too."

When Peggy became interested in patchworking a while ago she gifted her knitting needle collection to Kristy, but recently she's been asking for the needles back, as she is taking up knitting again.

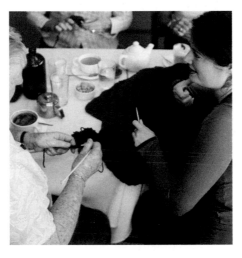

For most of us, 'Help Desk', means the person we call when computer problems arise, however Kristy's personal knitting 'Help Desk' is her Nanna, who is only a phone call away.

"It always surprises me that Nanna understands what I'm doing when I explain the problem in hand. She is able to picture the work in progress and advise if the yarn should be forward or back or how to slip a stitch. It's as though she can see the work on my needles," Kristy says.

The theme of sharing knowledge resonates throughout our discussion. As well as practising accountancy, Kristy teaches it, deriving great satisfaction from ensuring that all her students receive a better deal than she did when she was studying accountancy. And after many years of classical ballet, teaching dance has also been incorporated into the mix. Kristy says that after more than a decade of dance, she finds enjoyment in passing on skills she has picked up, and she gets the same enjoyment from sharing her knitting skills.

Knitting has been the glue for keeping generations of family and friends together in Kristy's circle. In recent times a winter knitting group was begun amongst the 'younguns' with the idea of starting a new project at the beginning of winter and helping each other to work through any knitting problems whilst sharing a glass of wine or three.

"We had in mind a hip young gathering, but everybody wanted their mums to come along, for one reason or another, and so it's really become a mother and daughter club," Kristy said. "Relationships between most of us date back to high school when mums were taking us to dancing and we all saw a lot of each other during practice and productions. It's really just an extension of those times."

The next project Kristy is planning is a luxurious winter dressing gown for a friend. When I asked her to describe the gown she explained that she hadn't designed it yet, but she had in mind to use a generous cardigan wrap pattern as a base, and then to extend the collar and shorten the sleeves, "so they don't drag in the breakfast cereal" and to use a luxurious DK weight pink tweed yarn.

"Balance" was cited by Kristy as a benefit that knitting brings.

"It's become my retreat and a way to turn my thoughts away from work at the end of the day."

She explained how her knitting creates a space for creativity, of a different kind from accounting, providing the environment for taking on challenge and testing new skills without any real risk.

"The worst that can happen is I have to pull back the work and start again, but I like the feeling I get when I complete the project and it works."

knitting fits

When you consider the pleasure and fulfilment knitting can bring, it's not hard to get your head around the new trend, but what triggered knitting's recent popularity?

With an eclectic mix lining up for wool at the local yarn store, knitting knows no boundaries. The usual suspects are about to take it up, or already have. . . pop stars, bus drivers, latte sipping metrosexuals and anybody's husband, sister or aunt, even a few felines have been seen playing with a ball of yarn. City professionals and sea-changers of both sexes are incorporating knitting into their work and play, adding a sense of balance and ease to the daily grind. They do it at home, at work, in transit and on holiday. On-the-train knitting is a phenomenon that was, until recently, considered a grandma activity, but has now become acceptable. . . it's hip! Cafe and pub knitting clubs are the norm, rather than the exception and projects-of-choice are often small portable items for gift giving.

When you consider the pleasure and fulfilment knitting can bring, its not hard to get your head around the new trend, but what triggered knitting's new popularity?

It had practically disappeared in the early 80's, but resurfaced, almost immediately post 9/11 when the world stopped for a moment and we took account of our lives and what was more important to us: fast paced achievements in the workplace or time spent enriching self and family? Since then we've embraced knitting for the haven it provides.

And how interesting that, despite its beginnings as an antidote to technology, "neo-knitting" has merged seamlessly with it. Yesterday's knitter used pattern book and yarn store as a resource, while today's knitter moves easily between website, store and print. This connection between knitting and modern technology increases the relevance of the craft to a new young market and there are thousands of web sites around the world available for immediate help at home. Sites such as www.studioknits.com and www.stitchguide.com offer help to amateur and experienced knitters alike. Another wonderful site, which hosts mesmerising animated knitting technique pages, is at www.dnt-inc.com. There is also an immense world knitting community who chat regularly on-line and exchange experiences about yarn, patterns, and just about everything else, from sex in hand knitted socks to preferences for music (while knitting) and career choices, in between knitting projects of course!

So what else is driving the trend? The simplicity and portability of knitting **creates a resonance with other "in-the-moment" pursuits such as meditation and yoga,** endearing it to a generation striving for balance. Whilst the craft of dressmaking requires a sophisticated machine, a desk and space in your home, knitting is completely transportable, can be popped into a bag and produced for getting on with anywhere, anytime. It is an age old craft in a new age world perhaps akin only to weaving, where a fabric is hand made from a thread using primitive tools.

It's about empowerment and self-made style, not slavishly following fashion. Once upon a time, when choices were few and questioning was not encouraged, it was not the done thing to make changes, however in today's (western) world, life revolves around change, choice and the freedom to explore everything and anything. So it's natural that today's knitters are encouraged to pursue their craft with questioning and with the

Knitting websites:
www.studioknits.com
www.stitchguide.com
www.dnt-inc.com

... the process of making a wearable item with simple tools and yarn becomes a way of life for a while.

confidence to make changes. **Once happy to copy a design, knitters today are more inclined to create a fabric or garment design through experimentation**, or to personalise a published design by making changes to colours and textures.

The notion that the craft is contributing to a revolution amongst the 'time poor' classes in today's turbulent environment may not be as far fetched as it sounds. As we engage with knitting and take time to reflect, we simultaneously allow ourselves space to formulate new ways of being and to revise our perspective about the part we play in the world. To create a piece of cloth from its very beginnings is a way of threading together days and weeks.

What better gift to give than something made from a fibre of your own choice and with the skill of your own hands. Such a wonderful alternative to the perennial routine of rushing around and buying an obligatory gift. A story unfolds while the project grows, the choice of yarn and pattern, the chair on the sunny patio where you knitted, mistakes made and the friendly interaction with by-standers as they show an interest in your work. Skills are learned and the process of making a wearable item with simple tools and yarn becomes a way of life for a while. **The project you knit becomes a tangible link in the future to the things that were happening in your life at the time of knitting.** A self affirming craft that brings satisfaction and joy.

The novelty of casting on to knit began as a craze just a few short years back and has now been comfortably integrated into the lifestyles of many. Knitting will be here for the long run because of the enduring qualities of the craft. Infinite variations are possible when playing with colour, fibre, fabric and design. It's an accessible indulgence which brings counterbalance to the hurried excesses of living in today's technologically driven society. Once picked up and learned, knitting stays for a lifetime. To knit, to contemplate and finally to share the fruit of your labour, brings its own rewards.

knit 'n' purl stitches

If you can knit and purl, you can make these classic stitch pattern fabrics. Knit 'samplers' in colours that harmonize and join together to create a throw or cushion cover. Choose patterns and yarns that match when measured for tension, so that the finished project will easily fit together. Page 105 explains how to measure tension.

2 STITCH RIB

MULTIPLE OF 4 + 2
1st Row: K2, *P2, K2; rep from * to end.
Rep this row.

4 STITCH RIB

MULTIPLE OF 8 + 4
1st Row K4, *P4, K4; rep from * to end.
Rep this row.

HORIZONTAL DASH STITCH

MULTIPLE OF 10 + 6
1st Row (RS) P6, *K4, P6; rep from * to end.
2nd and every alt row Purl.
3rd Row Knit.
5th Row P1, *K4, P6; rep from * to last 5 sts, K4, P1.
7th Row Knit.
8th Row Purl.
Rep thes 8 rows.

GARTER STITCH CHECKS

MULTIPLE OF 10 + 5
1st Row (RS) K5, *P5, K5; rep from * to end.
2nd Row Purl.
Rep the last 2 rows once more then the 1st row again.
6th Row K5, * P5, K5; rep from * to end.
7th Row Knit.
Rep the last two rows once more then the 6th row again.
Rep these 10 rows.

DOUBLE FLECK STITCH

MULTIPLE OF 6 + 4
1st & 3rd Rows (RS) Knit.
2nd Row P4, *K2, P4; rep from * to end.
4th Row P1, *K2, P4; rep from * to last 3 sts, K2, P1.
Rep these 4 rows.

CHEQUERBOARD

MULTIPLE OF 8 + 4
1st Row K4, *P4, K4; rep from * to end.
2nd Row P4, * K4, P4; rep from * to end.
Rep the last two rows once more.
5th Row As 2nd Row.
6th Row As 1st Row.
Rep the last two rows once more.
Rep these 8 rows.

DIAMOND BROCADE

MULTIPLE OF 8 + 1
1st Row (RS) K4, *P1, K7; rep from * to last 5 sts, P1, K4.
2nd Row P3, *K1, P1, K1, P5; rep from * to last 6 sts, K1, P1, K1, P3.
3rd Row K2, *P1, K3; rep from * to last 3 sts, P1, K2.
4th Row P1, *K1, P5, K1, P1; rep from * to end.
5th Row *P1, K7; rep from * to last st, P1.
6th Row As 4th Row.
7th Row As 3rd Row.
8th Row As 2nd Row. Rep these 8 rows.

japanese
katazome

by Sue Leighton-White

A trip to Japan for a textile enthusiast is not complete until a flea market is visited. The main markets are in Tokyo and Kyoto, but those held in smaller towns and cities are often where fewer western people visit and the more exciting textiles are found.

Above and opposite top left, centre, and bottom left, a selection of traditional katazome fabrics.
Opposite, bottom centre, a 'katagami' paper stencil.
Opposite Top right, a Japanese painting showing a kimono with katazome fabric.
Opposite bottom right, A contemporary fabric using traditional katazome motifs.

Theodore Manning's 2003 book, 'Flea Markets of Japan', lists 115 flea market sites, but there are even more to be found through the local tourist office.

Some of the more spectacular textiles to be found are the bed quilt covers, sold in strips or quilt tops. The designs, which remain undyed on an indigo background, are timeless, traditional and of infinite variety. The fabric is dyed using a method called 'katazome' or stencil dyeing.

Katazome uses cut stencils called 'katagami', to provide the designs It is well suited to mass production since the same stencil is moved along the fabric after the rice-resist paste has been applied. If it is a simple two-colour design, as seen in many indigo and cream fabrics, only one stencil needs to be cut. Where there are several colours on the fabric, a different stencil is cut for each colour.

The stencils are made with layers of paper from the paper mulberry plant, glued together, then strengthened with persimmon juice, smoked, then cut with precision instruments into the finest designs. For each different type of cut made on the paper, a different tool is used. Thus a circle is cut with a stencil cutter that has a circle at the base, and a square is cut with a square-based cutter.

After the rice resist is applied through the stencil, it is left to dry, then sized with an extract of soybean liquid. The fabric is immersed in the dye bath a number of times. After several days the dyed material is soaked in water to remove the resist paste.

This type of dyeing was used for different items. As well as being used for bed quilt covers, it was a means of making kimono fabric for commoners unable to wear the more elaborate fabrics of their superiors. Historically, clothing was tightly controlled in design and colour, with the Edo period (1600-1868) sumptuary laws confining bright colours and bold designs to kimono linings and kimono undergarments.

Where the katazome technique was used to dye small all-over designs, it was called komon. Medium size designs were called chugata. Quite different to the restrained komon designs, they showed a freedom in the choice of images from nature. Today, the more expensive summer yukatas are still made with the katazome technique, with chugata designs.

Today katazome is found in antique shops and flea markets, mostly in the form of indigo and cream bed quilt covers, both elegant and simple. There are more of these surviving, probably due to the heavier cotton used, than the komon and chugata style kimonos from the past, which often are only found as fragments.

The bed quilt covers show an amazing ability to overcome the limitation of the carved stencil, just as the kimono shape is a limiting structure to which creativity has given a never-ending variety of designs.

The quilt cover designs are timeless, and have continued to be used to this day, as source material for contemporary printed fabrics.

This japanese quilted fabric tote,
make it and take it with you.

tokyo tote

This light and soft quilted carry bag is easy to make.
A comfortable carrying companion for knitters on the move.

MATERIALS

Quilted fabric - 70cm (108cm wide).
Navy fabric - 30cm (112cm wide).
Sewing thread to match fabrics.

TOOLS

Fabric marking pencil, sewing pins, tape
measure, sharp fabric cutting scissors.
Rotary cutter and cutting board (optional).
Sewing machine in good working order.

CUTTING

Navy fabric:
Cut 2 pieces 9cm x 50cm
Cut 2 pieces 9cm x 75cm
Quilted fabric:
Cut 1 piece 50cm x 90cm
Cut 2 pieces 5cm x 75cm

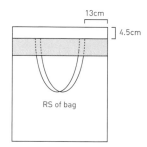

13cm
4.5cm
RS of bag

Tokyo Tote kits are available from:

Sanshi
115 Palmerston St,
Mosman Park,
Western Australia 6012

Phone/Fax: +61 8 9431 7336

Website: www.sanshi.com.au

ASSEMBLY

Handles To bind the long cut edges of the
handles, take one of each of the 9cm x 75cm
navy and 5cm x 75cm quilted fabric pieces,
and with right sides together, machine stitch
along the edge.
Press with a warm iron on the stitching
on the navy fabric side.
Fold the navy fabric over the raw edge and
the back of the quilted fabric handle and
press. Fold over the edge of the navy fabric
1cm towards wrong side of fabric and press.
Bring this folded edge over the remaining
raw edge to the right side of the quilted
handle and machine sew in place.
Repeat for second handle.
NB: Alternate the direction when sewing
on these long edges to prevent warping
and stretching of the handles.
Attach handles to bag With the right sides
of both bag fabric and handles facing, position
handles as indicated by the diagram.
Take a 9cm x 50cm piece of navy fabric and
pin in position over the bag handles and
machine stitch across the top.
Press along the machine sewing before lifting
the navy fabric and the handles toward the top
of the bag. Press. Machine stitch across the
bag 0.5cm in from the folded edge of the navy
fabric and handles.
Fold over the edge of the navy fabric.
Fold the navy fabric over the raw edge
to the inside of the bag, pin in place.
Machine stitch along this edge and at the
same time sewing across the bag handles.
Repeat at other end.
With the right sides of the bag together,
sew along the sides of the bag, backstitching
at the top to give it strength.
To create a corner for the bag, press open
side seams. Align the middle of the side seam
with the fold at the bottom of the bag.
With the right sides of the fabric together,
pin and machine stitch across corner.
Trim across and neaten raw edges with
an overlocker or zig zag machine stitch.

general pattern instructions

TENSION

At the start of each pattern, the required tension is given. Before beginning, it is most important to check your tension. Refer to page 105 for instructions on how to knit a tension square.

YARN QUANTITIES

Yarn quantities given are approximate estimations based on average requirements using specified tension and Jo Sharp yarn.

READING GRAPHS

Each square on a graph represents one stitch. Unless otherwise stated, graphs are worked in Stocking stitch. When working from a graph, read odd rows (RS) from right to left and even rows (WS) from left to right. Graphs may be enlarged by photocopy for easier reading.

COLOUR REPRODUCTION

Inaccuracies of some illustrated yarn shades in this book are caused by photographic and printing reproduction processes that are unavoidable. To avoid disappointment, it is advisable to view an actual yarn sample before purchasing yarn.

CARING FOR YOUR GARMENT

HAND WASHING

For the best result gently hand wash in lukewarm water, using a wool detergent. Rinse thoroughly in lukewarm water. Rinse again in cold water.

DRYING

To remove excess moisture after washing, roll inside a large towel and gently squeeze. Alternatively, spin dry inside a pillow case. Never tumble dry. Place on a flat surface in the shade to dry, coaxing it back into shape whilst damp. Drying flat is recommended. Do not dry directly in front of an open or artificial fire.

DRY CLEANING

Generally is not recommended as residual dry cleaning chemicals tend to harden hand knitted fabric.

PATTERN QUERIES

Jo Sharp Hand Knitting Yarns
PO Box 1018, Fremantle WA 6959
Phone: +61 8 9430 9699
Fax: +61 8 9430 9499
Email: yarn@josharp.com.au
Website: www.josharp.com.au

ABBREVIATIONS

alt	alternate
beg	beginning
ch	chain
circ	circular
cn	cable needle
cm	centimetres
col	colour
cont	continue
dc	double crochet
dec	decrease
foll	follow/ing
htr	half treble
in	inch/es
inc	increase
incl	including
K	knit
Kb1	Knit into the back of stitch
Kfb	Increase by knitting into front and back of K stitch
K2tog	Knit 2 stitches together
K2tog-b	Knit 2 together through back of stitch
M1	Make 1. Pick up loop between sts and knit into back of it
mm	millimetres
patt	pattern
P	purl
Pbf	Increase by purling into back and front of P stitch
psso	pass slip stitch over
rem	remain/ing
rep/s	repeat/s
rev	reverse/ing
rnd	round
RS	right side
sl	slip
sl st	slip stitch
st/s	stitch/es
St st	Stocking stitch
tbl	through back of loop
tog	together
tr	treble
vers	version
WS	wrong side
yb	yarn back
yf	yarn forward
yfon	yarn forward and over needle
yon	yarn over needle
yrn	yarn round needle
yrs	years

METRIC TO IMPERIAL CONVERSION

cm	in	cm	in
1	$^3/_8$	15	6
1.5	$^5/_8$	15.5	$6^1/_8$
2	$^7/_8$	16	$6^3/_8$
2.5	1	16.5	$6^5/_8$
3	$1^1/_4$	17	$6^3/_4$
3.5	$1^3/_8$	17.5	$6^7/_8$
4	$1^1/_2$	18	$7^1/_8$
4.5	$1^3/_4$	18.5	$7^1/_4$
5	2	19	$7^1/_2$
5.5	$2^1/_8$	19.5	$7^3/_4$
6	$2^3/_8$	20	8
6.5	$2^9/_{16}$	25	10
7	$2^3/_4$	30	12
7.5	3	35	$13^3/_4$
8	$3^1/_4$	40	16
8.5	$3^3/_8$	45	18
9	$3^5/_8$	50	$19^3/_4$
9.5	$3^3/_4$	55	22
10	4	60	$23^3/_4$
10.5	$4^1/_8$	65	25
11	$4^3/_8$	70	28
11.5	$4^1/_2$	75	$29^1/_2$
12	$4^3/_4$	80	$31^1/_2$
12.5	5	85	$33^1/_2$
13	$5^1/_8$	90	36
13.5	$5^5/_{16}$	95	38
14	$5^1/_2$	100	40
14.5	$5^3/_4$		

NEEDLE SIZE CONVERSION

mm	USA	UK
2	0	14
2.25	1	13
2.75	2	12
3		11
3.25	3	10
3.5	4	
3.75	5	9
4	6	8
4.5	7	7
5	8	6
5.5	9	5
6	10	4
6.5	10.5*	3
7	10.5*	2
7.5		1
8	11	0
9	13	00
10	15	000

*Depends on brand of needles

exciting preparations
for the day ahead

An afternoon inside wearing a snuggly poncho that you made yourself with wool, silk and cashmere yarn.

Above, Poncho, pattern on page 30.
Opposite, **Poncho** detail.

Above, **Beret**, pattern on page 31.
Above and opposite, **Wrap Cardigan**,
pattern on page 32.

Poncho

This cuddly poncho is worked with bold horizontal cables. The fringed edging is knitted separately and sewn in place.

Poncho

YARN

Colour	Quantity
Size	One size
Jo Sharp Silkroad Ultra x 50g balls	
707 Snow	10

NEEDLES

1 pair 7.00mm needles (USA 10.5) (UK 2).
1 6.50mm circular needle (USA 10.5) (UK 3).
1 cable needle.

MEASUREMENTS

Measurements given in inches are approximate.

Length - 48cm (19 in) without fringe.
Width (at lower edge) - 68cm (26³/₄ in).

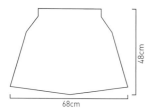

PATTERN

TENSION

13.5 sts and 16 rows measured over 10cm (approx 4 in) of St st using 7.00mm needles.

SPECIAL ABBREVIATIONS

C8B (Cable 8 back) - slip next 4 sts onto a cable needle and hold at back of work, knit next 4 sts from left hand needle, knit sts from cable needle.

FRONT AND BACK
Make 2

Using 7.00mm needles, cast on 52 sts.
Work side shaping (RS) K7, P1, K4, P2, K4, P1, K8, P1, K4, P2, K4, P1, K8, P1, K4.
(WS) P4, K1, P8, K1, P4, K2, P4, K1, P8, K1, P4, K2, P4, K1, P7.
(RS) Cast on 2 sts at beg of row, P1, C8B, P1, K4, P2, K4, P1, C8B, P1, K4, P2, K4, P1,C8B, P1, K4 (54 sts).
(WS) P4, K1, P8, K1, P4, K2, P4, K1, P8, K1, P4, K2, P4, K1, P8, K1.
(RS) Cast on 2 sts at beg of row, K2, P1, K8, P1, K4, P2, K4, P1, K8, P1, K4, P2, K4, P1, K8, P1, K4 (56 sts).
(WS) P4, K1, P8, K1, P4, K2, P4, K1, P8, K1, P4, K2, P4, K1, P8, K1, P2.
(RS) Cast on 2 sts at beg of row, K4, P1, K8, P1, K4, P2, K4, P1, K8, P1, K4, P2, K4, P1, K8, P1, K4 (58 sts).
(WS) P4, K1, P8, K1, P4, K2, P4, K1, P8, K1, P4, K2, P4, K1, P8, P4.
(RS) Cast on 6 sts at beg of row, K4, P2, K4, P1, K8, P1, K4, P2, K4, P1, K8, P1, P2, K4, P1, K8, P1, K4 (64 sts).
(WS): P4, K1, P8, K1, P4, K2, P4, K1, P8, K1, P4, K2, P4, K1, P8, K1, P4, K2, P4.
Working cable cross on next (RS) row, and every following 8th row, cont working in pattern for a further 31 rows, finishing on a RS row. Keeping patt and cable crosses correct, work short rows to shape centre front as follows:
(WS) Patt to last 5 sts, * sl and wrap yarn over slipped st, turn**.

(RS) Patt this and all RS rows whilst working short row shaping.
(WS) Patt to last st, rep fom * to **
(WS) Patt to last 5 sts, rep from * to **.
(WS) Patt to last 9 sts, rep from * to **.
(WS) Patt to last 6 sts, rep from * to **.
(WS) Patt to last 5 sts, rep from * to **.
(WS) Patt to last 9 sts, rep from * to **.
(WS) Patt to last 6 sts, rep from * to **.
(WS) Patt to last 5 sts, rep from * to **.
(WS) Patt to last 5 sts, rep from * to **.
(WS) Patt across all sts, knitting short row wraps together with wrapped st to hide. Start rev short row shaping. Patt RS row.
(WS) Patt 5 sts, rep from * to **.
(WS) Patt 14 sts, rep from * to **.
(WS) Patt 19 sts, rep from * to **.
(WS) Patt 25 sts, rep from * to **.
(WS) Patt 34 sts, rep from * to **.
(WS) Patt 39 sts, rep from * to **.
(WS) Patt 45 sts, rep from * to **.
(WS) Patt 59 sts, rep from * to **.
(WS) Patt 60 sts, rep from * to **.
Cont working in patt without shaping for a further 33 rows, finishing with a WS row.
Work side shaping (RS) Keeping patt correct on rem sts,cast off 6 sts at beg of this row and then 2 sts at beg of next 3 (RS) rows (52 sts). Patt last row (WS). Cast off.

MAKING UP

Press pieces gently, using a warm iron over a damp cloth. Join side seams.
Neckband With RS facing, using 6.50mm circ needle, pickup and K 68 sts evenly along front edge and 68 sts evenly along back edge [136 sts]. Work in rounds of K2, P2 rib for 5cm, cast off in rib.

PICOT EDGING

Using 7.00mm needles, cast on 5 sts.
*Cast off 4 sts, slip remaining st on right hand needle, cast on 4 sts; rep from * until length is sufficient to cover bottom edge of poncho. Sew into place.

Beret

Beret

A shaped beret worked in Stocking stitch with a ribbed band.

YARN

Colour	Quantity
Size	One size

Jo Sharp Silkroad Aran Tweed x 50g balls

| 142 Taffeta | 1 |

NEEDLES

1 pair 4.50mm needles (USA 7) (UK 7).
1 pair 5.00mm needles (USA 8) (UK 6).

MEASUREMENTS

One size fits all.

PATTERN

TENSION

18 sts and 24 rows measured over 10cm (approx 4 in) of St st using 5.00mm needles.

BERET

Using 4.50mm needles, cast on 88 sts. Work in K2, P2 rib for 6 rows, inc 1 st at end of last row [89 sts].
(RS) (inc) (K3, Kfb on next st) 22 times, K1 [111 sts].
Change to 5.00mm needles.
Work 7 rows in St st.
Shape Top Row 1 (RS) (inc) (K5, Kfb on next st) 18 times, K3 [129 sts].
Work 9 rows in St st.
Row 11 (RS) (dec) (K4, K2tog) 21 times, k3 [108 sts].
Work 7 rows.
Row 19 (RS) (K9, K3tog) 9 times [90 sts].
Work 3 rows.
Row 23 (RS) (K8, K2tog) 9 times [81 sts].
Work 1 row.
Row 25 (RS) (K6, K2tog) 10 times, K1 [71 sts].
Work 1 row.
Row 27 (RS) (K5, K2tog) 10 times, K1 [61 sts].
Work 1 row.
Row 29 (RS) (K3, K3tog) 10 times, K1 [41 sts].
Work 1 row.
Row 31 (RS) (K3tog) 13 times, K2tog [14 sts].
Break yarn, thread through rem 14 sts and draw tog firmly and secure. Join seam.

Wrap Cardigan

A comfy wrap cable cardigan with tie belt.
The shawl collar is worked in 2 x 2 rib.

Wrap Cardigan

Colour	Quantity			
Size	A	B	C	D
Jo Sharp Silkroad Aran Tweed x 50g balls				
144 Willow	15	17	17	18

1 pair 4.50mm needles (USA 7) (UK 7).
1 pair 5.00mm needles (USA 8) (UK 6).
1 cable needle.

Measurements given in inches are approximate.

Women's Sizing	A	B	C	D
To fit bust				
cm	80	90	100	110
in	31$\frac{1}{2}$	35$\frac{1}{2}$	39$\frac{1}{2}$	43$\frac{1}{2}$
Bodice circumference				
cm	92	104	116	130
in	36$\frac{1}{4}$	41	45$\frac{3}{4}$	51$\frac{1}{4}$
Bodice length				
cm	70	70	72	72
in	27$\frac{1}{2}$	27$\frac{1}{2}$	28$\frac{1}{2}$	28$\frac{1}{2}$
Sleeve length				
cm	44	44	46	46
in	17$\frac{1}{4}$	17$\frac{1}{4}$	18	18

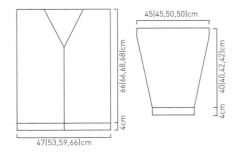

PATTERN

TENSION

18 sts and 24 rows measured over 10cm (approx 4 in) St st using 5.00mm needles. Cable Panel measures 10.5cm.

SPECIAL ABBREVIATIONS

T4L (Twist 4 Left) - slip next 3 sts onto cable needle and hold at front of work, purl next st from left hand needle, then knit sts from cable needle.

T4R (Twist 4 Right) - slip next st onto cable needle and hold at back of work, knit next 3 sts from left hand needle, then purl st from cable needle.

C6F (Cable 6 Front) - slip next 3 sts onto cable needle and hold at front of work, knit next 3 sts from left hand needle, then knit sts from cable needle.

C6B (Cable 6 Back) - slip next 3 sts onto cable needle and hold at back of work, knit next 3 sts from left hand needle, then knit sts from cable needle.

C4B or C4F (Cable 4 Back or Front) - slip next 2 sts onto cable needle and hold at back (or front) of work, knit next 2 sts from left hand needle, then knit sts from cable needle.

CABLE 1
(4 sts)
Row 1 (RS) Knit.
Row 2 Purl.
Row 3 C4F.
Row 4 Purl.   Repeat these 4 rows.

CABLE 2
(4 sts)
Row 1 (RS) Knit.
Row 2 Purl.
Row 3 C4B.
Row 4 Purl.   Repeat these 4 rows.

CABLE 3
(36 sts)
Row 1 (RS) P6, T4L, T4R, P8, T4L, T4R, P6.
Row 2 K7, P6, K10, P6, K7.
Row 3 P7, C6F, P10, C6F, P7.
Row 4 As row 2.
Row 5 P6, T4R, T4L, P8, T4R, T4L, P6.
Row 6 K6, P3, K2, P3, K8, P3, K2, P3, K6.
Row 7 P5, T4R, P2, T4L, P6, T4R, P2, T4L, P5.
Row 8 K5, P3, K4, P3, K6, P3, K4, P3, K5.
Row 9 P5, K3, P4, T4L, P4, T4R, P4, K3, P5.
Row 10 K5, P3, K5, P3, K4, P3, K5, P3, K5.
Row 11 P5, T4L, P4, T4L, P2, T4R, P4, T4R, P5.
Row 12 K6, P3, K5, P3, K2, P3, K5, P3, K6.
Row 13 P6, T4L, P4, T4L, T4R, P4, T4R, P6.
Row 14 K7, P3, K5, P6, K5, P3, K7.
Row 15 P7, T4L, P4, C6B, P4, T4R, P7.
Row 16 K8, P3, K4, P6, K4, P3, K8.
Row 17 P8, (T4L, P2, T4R) twice, P8.
Row 18 K9, P3, (K2, P3) 3 times, K9.
Row 19 P9, T4L, T4R, P2, T4L, T4R, P9.
Row 20 K10, P6, K4, P6, K10.
Row 21 P10, C6F, P4, C6F, P10.
Row 22 As row 20.
Row 23 P9, T4R, T4L, P2, T4R, T4L, P9.
Row 24 As row 18.
Row 25 P8, (T4R, P2, T4L) twice, P8.
Row 26 As row 16.
Row 27 P7, T4R, P4, C6B, P4, T4L, P7.
Row 28 As row 14.
Row 29 P6, T4R, P4, T4R, T4L, P4, T4L, P6.
Row 30 As row 12.
Row 31 P5, T4R, P4, T4R, P2, T4L, P4, T4L, P5.
Row 32 As row 10.
Row 33 P5, K3, P4, T4R, P4, T4L, P4, K3, P5.
Row 34 As row 8.
Row 35 P5, T4L, P2, T4R, P6, T4L, P2, T4R, P5.
Row 36 As row 6.   Repeat these 36 rows.

LEFT FRONT

Using 4.50mm needles, cast on 56(60,66,72) sts. Work in K2, P2 rib for 4cm, ending on a WS row and inc 1 st each end last row worked [58(62,68,74) sts]. Change to 5.00mm needles.

Establishment rows:

Row 1 (RS) P7(9,12,15) sts, work Row 1 Cable 1, work Row 1 Cable 3, work Row 1 Cable 2, P7(9,12,15) sts.

Row 2 K7(9,12,15) sts, work Row 2 Cable 2, work Row 2 Cable 3, work Row 2 Cable 1, K7(9,12,15) sts. These 2 rows set pattern. Cont working in patt as set until length measures 45(45,47,47)cm (incl band)*, ending on a RS row.

Shape Front Neck (WS) Dec 1 st at beg next row, then 1 st every alt row 5 times, then 1 st at neck edge every 3rd row 14(14,16,16) times [38(42,46,52) sts, 53(53,59,59) shaping rows]. Work 7(7,1,1) rows straight. Cast off.

RIGHT FRONT

Work as for Left Front to *, ending on a WS row. Cont working as for Left Front to end, rev all shaping.

BACK

Using 4.50mm needles, cast on 110(120,132,144) sts.
Work in K2, P2 rib for 4cm, ending on a WS row and inc 4 sts on last row worked [114(124,136,148) sts].
Change to 5.00mm needles.

Establishment rows

Row 1 (RS)

Size A P7, Row 1 Cable 1, Row 1 Cable 3, Row 1 Cable 2, P4, Row 1 Cable 2, P4, Row 1 Cable 1, Row 1 Cable 3, Row 1 Cable 1, P7.

Size B P9, Row 1 Cable 1, Row 1 Cable 3, Row 1 Cable 2, P7, Row 1 Cable 2, P7, Row 1 Cable 1, Row 1 Cable 3, Row 1 Cable 1, P9.

Size C P12, Row 1 Cable 1, Row 1 Cable 3, Row 1 Cable 2, P6, Row 1 Cable 1, P4, Row 1 Cable 2, P6, Row 1 Cable 2, Row 1 Cable 3, Row 1 Cable 1, P12.

Size D P15, Row 1 Cable 1, Row 1 Cable 3, Row 1 Cable 2, P9, Row 1 Cable 1, P4, Row 1 Cable 2, P9, Row 1 Cable 2, Row 1 Cable 3, Row 1 Cable 1, P15.

Row 2 (WS)

Size A K7, Row 2 Cable 1, Row 2 Cable 3, Row 2 Cable 1, K4, Row 2 Cable 2, K4, Row 2 Cable 2, Row 2 Cable 3, Row 2 Cable 1, K7.

Size B K9, Row 2 Cable 1, Row 2 Cable 3, Row 2 Cable 1, K7, Row 2 Cable 2, K7, Row 2 Cable 2, Row 2 Cable 3, Row 2 Cable 1, K9.

Size C K12, Row 2 Cable 1, Row 2 Cable 3, Row 2 Cable 2, K6, Row 2 Cable 2, K4, Row 2 Cable 1, K6, Row 2 Cable 2, Row 2 Cable 3, Row 2 Cable 1, K12.

Size D K15, Row 2 Cable 1, Row 2 Cable 3, Row 2 Cable 2, K9, Row 2 Cable 2, K4, Row 2 Cable 1, K9, Row 2 Cable 2, Row 2 Cable 3, Row 2 Cable 1, K15.

These 2 rows set pattern.
Cont working in patt as set until length measures same as fronts. Cast off.

SLEEVES

Using 4.50mm needles, cast on 48(48,52,52)sts. Work in K2, P2 rib for 4cm, ending on a WS row.
Change to 5.00mm needles.

Establishment rows:

Row 1 (RS) P2(2,4,4), work Row 1 Cable 1, Row 1 Cable 3, Row 1 Cable 2, P2(2,4,4).

Row 2 K2(2,4,4), work Row 2 Cable 2, Row 2 Cable 3, Row 2 Cable 1, K2(2,4,4).

These 2 rows set pattern.
Keeping patt correct, AT THE SAME TIME shape sides as follows; inc 1 st each end every 3rd row 4(4,13,13) times, then 1 st each end every 4th row 20(20,14,14) times [96(96,106,106) sts, 92(92,95,95) shaping rows].
Work straight until sleeve (incl band) measures 44(44,46,46)cm or length desired. Cast off.

MAKING UP

Press all pieces gently, except ribs, on WS using a warm iron over a damp cloth. Using Backstitch join shoulder seams. Centre sleeves and join, join side and sleeve seams using Edge to Edge st on ribs.

Bands With RS facing, using 4.50mm needles, pick up and knit 94 sts along right front from base to neck shaping. Work in P2, K2 rib for 15 rows.
Cast off in rib. Work left side as for right side, picking up from neck shaping to base.

Collar Using 4.50mm needles, cast on 150 sts. Work in K2, P2 rib for 15 rows. Cast off 3 sts at beg foll 36 rows. Cast off rem 42 sts in rib. Sew collar into position along cast off edge using Edge to Edge stitch.

Tie Belt Using 4.50mm needles, cast on 10 sts. Work in K1, P1 rib until length measures 170cm. Cast off.

Warmly wrapped
for a winter's day
of play.

Above and opposite, **Raglan Sweater**, pattern
on page 40. **Mohair Scarf** version 1, pattern on
page 39. **Rib Hat** version 1, pattern on page 41.

Snug and Hat

This snug top is worked sideways in Garter Rib pattern. The Stocking stitch hat features a 2x2 rib pattern at the base.

Snug and Hat

YARN

Colour	Quantity
Snug	
Size	**One size**
Jo Sharp Silkroad Ultra x 50g balls	
715 Seafoam	8
Hat	
Size	**One size**
Jo Sharp Silkroad Ultra x 50g balls	
715 Seafoam	2

NEEDLES

1 pair 6.50 mm needles (USA 10.5) (UK 3).

MEASUREMENTS

Measurements given in inches are approximate.

Snug
Width   110cm (43¼ in)
Length   35cm (13¾ in)

Hat
Circumference   46cm (18 in)

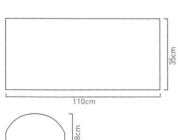

SNUG PATTERN

TENSION
14 sts and 20 rows measured over 10cm (approx 4 in) of Pattern using 6.50mm needles.

SNUG
Using 6.50mm needles, cast on 46 sts.
Row 1 K2, *P2, K2, rep from * to end.
Rep this row until length measures 110cm.
Cast off.

MAKING UP
With RS together, using Backstitch, join cast off row to cast on row, matching sts and keeping the seam flexible to allow some stretch.

HAT PATTERN

TENSION
14 sts and 20 rows measured over 10cm (approx 4 in) of St st using 6.50mm needles.

HAT
Using 6.50mm needles, cast on 70 sts.
Row 1 K2, *P2, K2, rep from * to end.
Row 2 P2, *K2, P2, rep from * to end.
Repeat these 2 rows 5 times [12 rows].
Knit next 2 rows.
Cont in St st until piece measures 13cm, ending on a knit row.
Next Row (WS) Dec 6 sts evenly across row [64 sts].
Next Row (RS) Knit.
Next Row (WS) *P2, P2tog; rep from * to end [48 sts].
Next Row (RS) Knit.
Next Row (WS) *P1, P2tog; rep from * to end [32 sts].
Next Row (RS) Knit.
Next Row (WS) *P2tog; rep from * to end [16 sts].
Rep last 2 rows.
Cast off rem 8 sts. Cut yarn, leaving enough thread to use for seam.

MAKING UP
With RS facing, draw cast off sts into a tight circle, then sew seam using Backstitch, matching rows.

Mohair Scarf

This kid mohair scarf is worked with a soft lace stitch, incorporating garter stitch stripes at intervals.

Mohair Scarf version 1

Mohair Scarf version 2

YARN

Version 1

Colour	Quantity
Size	One Size

Jo Sharp Rare Comfort Kid Mohair x 25g balls
609 Tranquil 4

Version 2

Colour	Quantity
Size	One Size

Jo Sharp Rare Comfort Kid Mohair x 25g balls
604 Foxglove 4

NEEDLES

1 pair 5.00mm needles (USA 8) (UK 6).

MEASUREMENTS

Measurements given in inches are approximate.

Version 1
Width – 30cm (12 in)
Length – 150cm (59 in)

Version 2
Width – 30cm (12 in)
Length – 100cm (39½ in)

Scarf Version 1
30cm
150cm

Scarf Version 2
30cm
100cm

SCARF PATTERN

TENSION
17 sts and 25 rows measured over 10cm (approx 4 in) of St st using 5.00mm needles.

SCARF
Using 5.00mm needles cast on 58 sts.
Rows 1 to 6 Knit.
Row 7 K1,* yon, K2, sl1, K2tog, psso, K2, yon, K1 * rep from * to last st, K1.
Rows 8 Purl.
Row 9 K1,* yon, K2, sl1, K2tog, psso, K2, yon, K1 * rep from * to last st, K1.
Row 10 Purl.
Row 11 K2tog,* K2, yon, K1, yon, K2, sl1, K2tog, psso * rep from * finishing with sl1, K1, psso, K1.
Row 12 Purl.
Row 13 K2tog,* K2, yon, K1, yon, K2, sl1, K2tog, psso * rep from * finishing with sl1, K1, psso, K1.
Row 14 Purl.
Rep from row 7 once more [22 rows].
These 22 rows form pattern repeat.
Cont working in patt until length measures 150cm for Version 1 or 100cm for version 2.
Work 6 rows Garter st. Cast off.
Fringe Cut strands of yarn 6cm in length. Using 4 strands tog, fold in half. Insert a crochet hook just above cast on (or off) edge from back to front. Catch the folded strands of yarn with the hook and pull through the knitting. Insert the ends of yarn into the loop and pull through to tighten. Cont in this way until edge is sufficiently covered with fringe. Trim ends to even lengths.
Repeat at other end.

Raglan Sweater

A cropped raglan sweater with a shaped bodice and an extra long 4 x 4 rib collar. Knitted with two yarns together.

Raglan Sweater

YARN

Colour	Quantity			
Size	A	B	C	D
Jo Sharp Silkroad Aran x 50g balls				
137 Empire	10	10	12	12
Jo Sharp Rare Comfort Kid Mohair x 25g balls				
609 Tranquil	10	10	10	12

NEEDLES

1 pair 7.00mm needles (USA 10.5) (UK 2).
1 5.00mm circular needle (USA 8) (UK 6).
1 6.00mm circular needle (USA 10) (UK 4).

MEASUREMENTS

Measurements given in inches are approximate.

Women's sizing	A	B	C	D
To fit bust				
cm	80	85	90	95
in	31½	33½	35½	37½
Bodice circumference				
cm	90	96	102	108
in	35½	37¾	40	42½
Bodice length				
cm	55	55	57	57
in	21½	21½	22½	22½
Sleeve length (seam)				
cm	48	48	48	48
in	19	19	19	19

20[20,22,22]cm
31cm
4cm
46(49,52,55)

20[20,22,22]cm
44cm
4cm
35(37,40,40)cm

PATTERN

TENSION

13 sts and 18 rows measured over 10cm (approx 4 in) of St st using 7.00mm needles using both yarns knitted together.

FRONT

Note: Garment is worked using Silkroad Aran and Rare Comfort Kid Mohair knitted together throughout.
Using 7.00mm needles, cast on 60(64,68,72) sts. Work in K4, P4 rib for 6 rows.
Now work in St st beg with a K row until length (incl band) measures 35cm, ending on a WS row.
Shape armholes (RS) Cast off 1(2,2,3) sts at beg next 2 rows.
Next row (RS) K4, K2tog, K to last 6 sts, K2tog tbl, K4.
Next row (WS) Purl.*
Rep last 2 rows 13(13,14,14) times [30(32,34,36) sts].
Shape neck (RS) K4, K2tog, K4(5,6,7) sts, turn, leave rem sts on a holder. Work each side of neck separately.
(WS) Cast off 3(3,3,4) sts, P to end.
(RS) K4, K2tog, K to end.
(WS) Cast off 2(2,3,3) sts, P to end.
(RS) K3(4,4,4) sts.
(WS) Cast off 2 sts, P1(2,2,2).
Size A (RS) Cast off rem st.
Sizes B, C, D (RS) K2tog.
(WS) Cast off rem st.
With RS facing, rejoin yarn to rem sts. Cast off 10 centre sts, K to last 6 sts, K2tog tbl, K4.
(WS) Purl.
(RS) Cast off 3(3,3,4) sts, K0(1,2,2) sts K2tog, K4.
(WS) Purl.
(RS) Cast off 2(2,3,3) sts, K3(4,4,4).
(WS) P1(2,2,2), P2tog tbl.
Size A (RS) Cast off rem st.
Sizes B, C, D (RS) K2tog, K1.
(WS) Cast off rem st.

BACK

Work as for front to *, rep 17(17,18,18) times, then rep dec row once more [20(22,24,26) sts]. Cast off.

SLEEVES

Using 7.00mm needles, cast on 32(32,36,36) sts. Work in K4, P4 rib for 6 rows.
Work 14 rows St st beg with a K row.
Now cont working in St st AT THE SAME TIME shape sides as foll: inc 1 st at each end of foll row, then 1 st each end foll 8th rows 6(7,7,7) times [46(48,52,52) sts, 49(57,57,57) shaping rows].
Cont working straight until length (incl band) measures 48cm, ending on a WS row.
Shape raglan Cast off 1(2,2,2) sts at beg next 2 rows.
Next row (RS) (dec) K4, K2tog, K to last 6 sts, K2tog tbl, K4.
Next row (WS) Purl.
Rep last 2 rows, 16(16,18,18) times [10 sts].
Next row (RS) K4, K2tog, K4.
(WS) Purl.
(RS) K3, K3tog, K3.
Cast off rem sts.

MAKING UP

Press all pieces gently on WS using a warm iron over a damp cloth. Using backstitch, join raglan seams. Join side and sleeve seams.
Neckband With RS facing, using 5.00mm circular needle, pickup 64(64,72,72) sts evenly around neck. Work 7 rounds of K4, P4 rib. Change to 6.00mm circular needle, cont working in rib until band measures 20cm. Cast off.

Rib Hat

These hats are worked in Stocking stitch using two yarns knitted together.

Rib Hat version 1

Rib Hat version 2

YARN

Colour	Quantity
Version 1	
Size	**One Size**
Jo Sharp Silkroad Aran x 50g balls	
Col A 137 Empire	1
Col C 101 Venetian	1
Jo Sharp Rare Comfort Kid Mohair x 25g balls	
Col B 609 Tranquil	1
Col D 602 Romany	1
Version 2	
Size	**One Size**
Jo Sharp Silkroad Aran x 50g balls	
Col A 103 Quartz	1
Jo Sharp Rare Comfort Kid Mohair x 25g balls	
Col B 604 Foxglove	1

NEEDLES

1 pair 6.00mm needles (USA 10) (UK 4).
1 pair 7.00mm needles (USA10.5) (UK 2).

MEASUREMENTS

Measurements given in inches are approximate.

Average Size
Circumference – 50cm.

24cm / 18cm

HAT PATTERN

TENSION
13 sts and 18 rows measured over 10cm (approx 4 in) of St st using 7.00mm needles.

HAT
Note: Hat is worked using Silkroad Aran and Rare Comfort Kid Mohair knitted together throughout.
Using 6.00mm needles and 1 strand each Col's C & D (vers 1) or A & B (vers 2), cast on 68 sts. Work in K2, P2 rib for 6cm, ending on a WS row.
Change to 7.00mm needles.
Now working in St st, change to Col's A & B (vers 1 only, vers 2 is worked in Col's A & B throughout). Work 6cm, ending on a WS row.
Change to Col's C & D (vers 1).
Shape top Row 1 (RS) K2tog, (K11, K2tog) 5 times, K1 [62 sts].
Row 2 Purl.
Row 3 K2tog, (K10, K2tog) to end [56 sts].
Row 4 Purl.
Row 5 K2tog, (K9, K2tog) to end [50 sts].
Row 6 Purl.
Row 7 Cont to dec 1 st less before dec's on every alt row, beg and ending with a dec until 32 sts rem.
Purl 1 row.
Next row (WS) K2tog; rep to end [16 sts].
Break yarn and thread through rem sts, pull thread tightly and secure.
Sew seam using Edge to Edge st.

create a sense
of occasion

Beautiful new pastel shades in Jo Sharp Rare Comfort Kid Mohair.

Light and refreshing is this mint green singlet made from kid mohair yarn.

Above and opposite, **Mohair Singlet** version 1, pattern on page 48.

Mohair Singlet

This little singlet has bodice shaping and knitted shoestring straps. Easy to make and light to wear.

Mohair Singlet version 1

Mohair Singlet version 2

YARN

Version 1

Colour	Quantity		
Size	A	B	C
Jo Sharp Rare Comfort Kid Mohair x 25g balls			
631 Apple	3	3	4

Version 2

Colour	Quantity		
Size	A	B	C
Jo Sharp Rare Comfort Kid Mohair x 25g balls			
609 Tranquil	3	3	4

NEEDLES

1 pair 4.00mm double pointed needles (USA 6) (UK 8).
1 pair 5.00mm needles (USA 8) (UK 6).

MEASUREMENTS

Measurements given in inches are approximate.

Women's sizing	A	B	C
Bust			
cm	85	90	95
in	33¹/₂	35¹/₂	37¹/₂
Bodice circumference			
cm	73	78	82
in	28³/₄	30³/₄	32¹/₄
Length			
cm	55	57	59
in	21³/₄	22¹/₂	23¹/₄

[Schematic diagram with measurements: 15cm, 4cm, 36(38,40)cm, 37.5(40,42)cm]

PATTERN

TENSION

17 sts and 25 rows measured over 10cm (approx 4 in) of St st using 5.00mm needles.

FRONT & BACK
Make 2

Using 5.00mm needles, cast on 64(68,72) sts. Work in St st throughout.
Dec 1 st at each end of 8th row, 5 times [54(58,62) sts], then inc 1 sts at each end of every 10th row, 4 times [62(66,70)sts].
Cont without further shaping until length measures 36(38,40)cm, ending on a WS row.
Shape armholes (RS) Cast off 3 sts at beg of next 2 rows.
(RS) Cast off 2 sts at beg of this and next 3 rows. Work 1 row without shaping, then dec 1 st at beg of next 2 rows [46(50,54) sts].
Work without further shaping until length measures 40(42,44)cm. Cast off.

MAKING UP

With RS facing, using edge to edge st, join side seams.
Straps (make 2) Using 4.00mm double pointed needles, cast on 4 sts. * K4, do not turn work, slide sts to right end of needle and pull yarn to tighten. Rep from * until length measures approx 30cm (or length required). Cast off. Sew straps to front and back at armhole edge.

Women's Sweater

A simple sweater with drop shoulder shaping and Stocking stitch collar made with tweed or mohair yarn.

Women's Sweater version 1

Women's Sweater version 2

YARN

Version 1

Colour	Quantity			
Size	A	B	C	D

Jo Sharp Silkroad Aran Tweed x 50g balls

138 Dove	9	10	11	12

Version 2

Colour	Quantity			
Size	A	B	C	D

Jo Sharp Rare Comfort Kid Mohair x 25g balls

604 Foxglove	9	10	11	12

NEEDLES

1 pair 4.50mm needles (USA 7) (UK 7).
1 pair 5.00mm needles (USA 8) (UK 6).
1 4.50mm circular needle (USA 7) (UK 7).
2 stitch holders.

MEASUREMENTS

Measurements given in inches are approximate.

Women's sizing	A	B	C	D
To fit bust				
cm	80	90	100	110
in	31½	35½	39½	43¼
Version 1 Bodice circumference				
cm	98	108	120	130
in	38½	42½	47¼	51¼
Version 2 Bodice circumference				
cm	104	116	126	138
in	41	45¾	49½	54¼
Bodice length				
cm	63	65	67	69
in	24¾	25½	26½	27¼
Sleeve length				
cm	45	47	48	50
in	17¾	18½	19	19¾

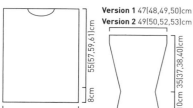

Version 1 47(48,49,50)cm
Version 2 49(50,52,53)cm

55(57,59,61)cm
8cm
10cm 35(37,38,40)cm

Version 1 50(55,61,66)cm
Version 2 53(59,64,70)cm

PATTERN

TENSION
Version 1
18 sts and 24 rows measured over 10cm (approx 4 in) of St st using 5.00mm needles.
Version 2
17 sts and 25 rows measured over 10cm (approx 4 in) of St st using 5.00mm needles.

BACK
Using 4.50mm needles, cast on 84(94,104,114) sts and work 21 rows in St st, ending on a RS row. Change to 5.00mm needles and start with a K row, inc 6 sts evenly across row [90(100,110,120) sts].*
Cont working in St st until work measures 63(65,67,69)cm incl band.
Shape back neck and shoulders (RS)
K35(40,45,50) sts, turn, leaving rem sts on a st holder.
(WS) Cast off 5 sts, P to end.
(RS) Knit.
(WS) Cast off 5 sts, P to end.
Cast off.
With RS facing, leave 20 sts on holder. Rejoin yarn to rem sts. Knit 1 row, then work second side to match first, rev all shaping.

FRONT
Work as for back to *.
Cont working in St st until work measures 57(59,61,63)cm incl band.
Shape front neck and shoulders (RS)
K35(40,45,50) sts, turn, leave rem sts on a st holder.
(WS) Cast off 2 sts at beg (neck edge) of this and next 4 WS rows. Work 8 more rows without shaping. Cast off.
With RS facing, leave 20 sts on holder. Rejoin yarn to rem sts. Knit 1 row, then work second side to match first, rev all shaping.

SLEEVES
Using 4.50mm needles, cast on 58(60,62,64) sts. Working in St st, dec 1 st at each end of Row 5 (RS), then every 4th row, 5 times [46(48,50,52) sts, 25 rows].

Change to 5.00mm needles and work in St st beg with a K row.
Shape Sleeve Inc 1 st at each end of every 4th row, 19 times [84(86,88,90) sts].
Cont without shaping until length measures 45(47,48,50)cm incl band or until length desired. Cast off.

MAKING UP
Press all pieces gently on WS using a warm iron over a damp cloth. Join shoulder seams, matching st to st.
Centre sleeves and join to armhole, matching 3 sts at top of sleeve to 4 rows on armhole edge. Join sleeve and side seams. Sew ends into seams.
Neckband With RS facing, using 4.50mm circular needle, pick up 18 sts down left side front neck, 20 sts from st holder, 18 sts along right side front neck, 10 sts along right side back neck, 20 sts from st holder and 10 sts along left side back neck. Work 30 rounds in St st with WS facing. Cast off.

Blow out the candles and make a wish in your favourite colours.

Above, **Children's Sweater**, pattern on page 58.
Opposite, **Women's Sweater** version 1, pattern on page 49.

It wouldn't
be a party
without
balloons!

Playful and
practical in
party mode.

Above, **Children's Sweater**, pattern on page 58.
Above right, **Cotton Scarf**, pattern on page 81.
Opposite, **Armings**, pattern on page 59.

Above, **Mohair Singlet** version 2, pattern on page 48.
Top left and opposite, **Leggings**, pattern on page 59.
Bottom left, swatches in **Silkroad Aran Tweed**.

comfy textures
for the great indoors

Children's Sweater

A simple cotton drop shoulder sweater knitted in Stocking stitch.

Children's Sweater

Colour	Quantity		
Size	3 - 5	6 - 8	9 - 11 yrs
Jo Sharp Desert Garden Aran Cotton x 50g balls			
237 Solstice	9	10	12

NEEDLES

1 pair 4.50mm needles (USA 7) (UK7).
1 pair 5.00mm needles (USA 8) (UK6).
2 stitch holders.

MEASUREMENTS

Measurements given in inches are approximate.

Children's sizing	3 - 5	6 - 8	9 - 11 yrs
To fit chest			
cm	57-64	64-74	74-84
in	22¹/₂-25¹/₄	25¹/₄-29	29-33
Bodice circumference			
cm	74	82	92
in	29	32¹/₄	36¹/₂
Bodice length			
cm	40	42	44
in	15³/₄	16¹/₂	17¹/₄
Sleeve length			
cm	31	34	37
in	12¹/₄	13¹/₂	14¹/₂

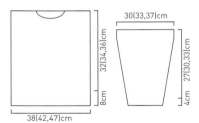

30(33,37)cm

32(34,36)cm

8cm

38(42,47)cm

27(30,33)cm

4cm

PATTERN

TENSION

18 sts and 24 rows measured over 10cm (approx 4 in) of St st using 5.00mm needles.

BACK

Using 4.50mm needles, cast on 68(76,84) sts. Work 19 rows St st, finishing on a RS row. Change to 5.00mm needles, and beg with a K row. Work another 70(76,82) rows St st, finishing on WS row.

Shape back neck (RS)
K29(32,35) sts, turn, leaving rem sts on a st holder.
(WS) Cast off 5 sts, P to end.
(RS) K to end.
(WS) Cast off 4 sts, P to end.
Work 2 rows without shaping, cast off rem 20(23,26) sts.
With RS facing, leave 10(12,14) centre sts on holder. Join yarn to rem sts.
K this row, then P next row.
(RS) Cast off 5 sts, K to end.
(WS) P to end.
(RS) Cast off 4 sts.
P next row, then cast off rem 20(23,26) sts.

FRONT

Work as for back to row 62(68,74).
Shape front neck (RS) K29(32,35) sts, turn, leaving rem sts on a st holder.
(WS) Cast off 2 sts at beg (neck edge) of this and next 2 foll WS rows, then cast off 1 st at neck edge on next 3 WS rows.
Work 2 rows without further shaping.
Cast off rem 20(23,26) sts.
With RS facing, leave 10(12,14) centre sts on a holder. Join yarn to rem sts.
K this row, then P next row.
(RS) Cast off 2 sts at beg (neck edge) of this and next 2 foll RS rows, then cast off 1 st at neck edge of next 3 RS rows.
Work 1 row, then cast off rem 20(23,26) sts.

SLEEVES

Using 4.50mm needles, cast on 36(38,40) sts. Working in St st beg with a K row, work 2 rows.
Dec 1 st at each end of next and foll K rows, 3 times (28(30,32) sts).
Work 2 rows, finishing with a K row.
Change to 5.00mm needles, cont in St st beg with a K row.
Work 4 rows finishing on a P row.
Shape sleeves (RS) Inc 1 st at each end of this and every 4th row 13(15,17) times (54(60,66) sts, 52(60,68) shaping rows).
Work 9 rows or until length desired. Cast off.

MAKING UP

Press all pieces gently on WS, using a warm iron over a damp cloth. With RS facing, using backstitch, join right shoulder seam.
Neckband With RS facing, using 4.50mm needles, pick up 10 sts down left side front neck, 10(12,14) sts from st holder on front neck, 10 sts along right side neck, 8 sts along right side back neck, 10(12,14) sts from st holder on back neck, and 8 sts along left side back neck (56(60,64) sts).
With WS facing, beg with a K row, work 10 rows St st. Cast off. Join second shoulder and neck seam. Centre sleeves then join. Join side and sleeve seams using edge to edge st.

Armings & Leggings

Both simply striped and ribbed top and bottom. Worked in the round using double pointed needles.

Armings

Leggings

YARN

Armings

Colour	Quantity
Size	One size

Jo Sharp Rare Comfort Kid Mohair x 25g balls
Col A 632 Twilight 2
Col B 630 Cloud 2

Leggings

Colour	Quantity
Size	One size

Jo Sharp Silkroad Aran Tweed x 50g balls
Col A 142 Taffeta 2
Col B 139 Spring 2

NEEDLES

1 set 4.50mm double pointed needles (USA 7) (UK 7).

MEASUREMENTS

One size fits average adult.

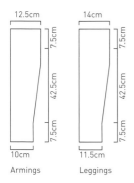

Armings   Leggings

PATTERN

TENSION
Armings
19.5 sts and 26 rows measured over 10cm (approx 4 in) of St st using 4.50mm needles.
Leggings
19 sts and 29 rows measured over 10cm (approx 4 in) of St st using 4.50mm needles.

COLOUR SEQUENCE
*2 rounds Col A.
2 rounds Col B.
Repeat from *.

ARMINGS & LEGGINGS
Make 2
Work in col sequence throughout.
Using 4.50mm needles and Col A, loosely cast on 52 sts. Divide onto 3 needles (18 sts, 16 sts, 18 sts).
Round 1 Rib Band *K2 tbl, P2, rep from * to end. Rep this round for 7.5cm.
Next Round Knit.
Rep this round for a further 17.5 cm.
Next Round Begin Shaping (dec) K1, K2tog, knit to last 3 sts, sl 1, K1, psso, K1.
Knit 5 rounds.
Rep last 6 rounds 3 times [44 sts].
Cont without shaping until work measures 50cm incl band.
Next Round Rib Band *K2tbl, P2; rep from * to end.
Rep this round for 7.5cm.
Cast off. Sew in ends.

the pleasure of
giving special things

Party in pink!

Embrace winter
with the warmth
of kid mohair.

Above, **Mohair Scarf** version 2, pattern on page 39.
Rib Hat version 2, pattern on page 41.
Opposite, **Women's Sweater** version 2, pattern on page 49.

Above and opposite, **Mohair Scarf** version 2,
pattern on page 39. Opposite, **Rib Hat** version 2,
pattern on page 41.

This is exactly
what I wished for,
my own rag doll
with her own outfit.

Above and opposite, **Dolly**, pattern on page 72.

Experiment with a palette of cool
pastels and earthy tones.
This children's sweater is worked
in intarsia with embroidery.

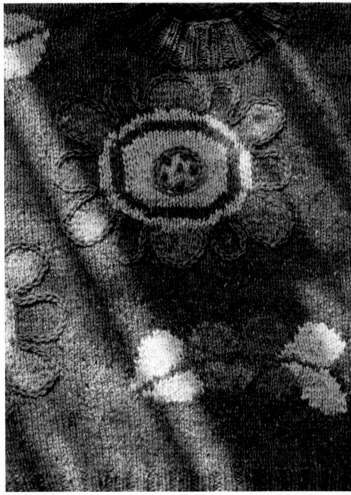

Top right and opposite, **Children's Intarsia Sweater**, pattern on page 73.
Top left (from left to right), **Silkroad DK Tweed** in 414 Autumn, 420 Eden, 412 Beanshoot.
Bottom (from left to right), **Silkroad Dk Tweed** in 418 Iceberg, 419 Butternut, 413 Pulp,
417 Snow, 416 Cocoa.

Dolly

This dolly has her own clothes that are knitted separately. A striped sweater, flared pants and a pinafore, all worked in Stocking stitch with a some simple embroidery to finish the look.

Dolly

Colour	Quantity
Size	One size
Jo Sharp Soho Summer DK Cotton x 50g balls	
Col A 227 Putty	1
Col B 230 Rockpool	1
Col C 219 Sailboat	1
Col D 234 Currant	1
Col E 222 Freesia	1
Col F 228 Calico	1

NEEDLES

1 pair 4.00mm needles (USA 6) (UK 8).

NOTIONS

Thin elastic.
Beads.
Filling.
Red and black yarn scraps for eyes and mouth.

MEASUREMENTS

Measurements given in inches are approximate.

Length - 50cm (19¾ in).

PATTERN

TENSION

22.5 sts and 30 rows measured over 10cm (approx 4 in) of St st using 4.00mm needles.

LEGS
(Make 2)

Using 4.00mm needles and Col A, cast on 24 sts and work 4 rows.
Next row (RS) K8, cast off 8 centre sts, K8.
Cont in St st, drawing the yarn tight across the gap made by cast off sts. Work 69 rows .
Cast off.

BODY AND HEAD
(Make 2)

Using 4.00mm needles and Col A, cast on 20 sts and work 28 rows, finishing with a WS row.
Shape shoulders and neck Cast off 3 sts at beg of next 4 rows [8 sts].
Work 6 rows for neck.
Face Row 1 Inc into 1st and 2nd sts, K3, inc into next 2 sts, K1 [12 sts].
Purl 1 row.
Row 3 Inc into 1st st, K9, inc into next st, K1 [14 sts].
Work 11 rows, ending with a WS row.
Row 15 K1, K2tog , K8, K2tog, K1.
Purl 1 row.
Row 17 K1, K2tog, K6, K2tog, K1.
Purl 1 row.
Row 19 K1, (K2tog, K1) 3 times.
Purl 1 row
Row 21 K1, K2tog 3 times. Cast off.

ARMS
(Make 2)

Using 4.00mm needles and Col A, cast on 12 sts and work 40 rows.
Next row (RS) K2tog to end. Cut yarn, secure sts by pulling thread through.

MAKING UP

Sew seams at front of foot. Join arm and leg seams, inserting filling before joining top seams. Join body and head seams, insert filling before joining last seam. Join arms to shoulder and legs to body. Embroider mouth and eyes.

HAIR

Using Col F, cut 60 lengths of 30cm. Centre strands on head and sew into position. Plait each side ands secure with a bow or little cord.

SWEATER

FRONT AND BACK
(Make 2)

Using 4.00mm needles and Col B, cast on 24 sts. Work 2 rows K1, P1 rib.
Work in Col sequence throughout as follows:
1 row Col C, 1 row Col D, 1 row Col B.
Using St st, work 24 rows.
Shape Neck
Next row (RS) K8, cast off 8 sts, K8.
(WS) P6, P2 tog, turn.
Cast off 7 sts.
With WS facing, rejoin yarn to rem 8 sts.
P2 tog, P6.
Cast off rem 7 sts.

SLEEVES
(Make 2)

Using 4.00mm needles and Col B, cast on 20 sts.
Work picot edge as follows.
Knit 1 row.
Purl 1 row.
K1, (K1, yon, K2tog) to end of row, K1.
Purl 1 row.
Knit, picking up st for st of cast on edge on wrong side, creating picot edge.
Cont working in St st and Col sequence.
Complete 24 rows. Cast off.

MAKING UP

Sew shoulder seams using backstitch.
Centre sleeves and join, then join side and sleeve seams.

PANTS
(Make 2)

Using 4.00mm needles and Col E, cast on 28 sts and work picot edge as on sleeves.
Cont working in St st, dec 1 st at each end next row, then on foll 6th row, then on foll 8th row, twice [20 sts].
Work 22 rows, finishing on a WS row.

Leave sts at end of needle, make another leg, then join both legs by knitting across all 44 sts. Work 22 rows in St st.

Waistband: Work 10 rows K1, P1 rib.
Cast off in rib.

MAKE UP

Join side and leg seams. Turn waistband back in half and slip st in place, leaving an opening for elastic. Thread elastic through waistband and st opening closed.

PINAFORE

FRONT AND BACK
(Make 2)

Using 4.00mm needles and Col D, cast on 56 sts and work picot edge as sleeves.
Cont working in St st, dec 1 st each end of next row, then 1 st each end foll 4th row, 7 times, then at each end of every 3rd row until 14 sts rem.
Work 6 more rows, finishing on a WS row.
Shape neck and armhole (RS) K5, cast off 4 sts, K4. Work each side separately.
*(WS) P3, P2tog.
(RS) K2tog, K2.
(WS) Purl 4.
(RS) K2tog, K1.
Cast off
Rep on other side from *, rev position of K2tog.

MAKING UP

Join side seams.
Make 4 cords for straps. Attach a bead to the end of each strap.

EMBROIDERY

Embroider pants and pinafore using lazy daisy stitch and french knots.

Children's Intarsia Sweater

This drop shoulder sweater features a floral design that is worked in Intarsia and embellished with embroidery.

Code	Colour	Quantity	
Size		5-6	7-8 yrs
Jo Sharp Silkroad DK Tweed x 50g balls			
Col A ☐	415 Festival	5	6
■	413 Pulp	1	1
+	412 Beanshoot	1	1
✓	404 Boheme	1	1

1 pair 3.75mm needles (USA 5) (UK9).
1 pair 4.00mm needles (USA 6) (UK 8).
2 stitch holders.

Measurements given in inches are approximate.

Children's sizing	5-6	7-8 yrs
To fit chest		
cm	62 - 66	67-71
in	24¹/₂-26	26¹/₂-28
Bodice circumference		
cm	82	92
in	32¹/₄	36¹/₄
Bodice length		
cm	49	55
in	19¹/₄	21³/₄
Sleeve length		
cm	29	31
in	11¹/₂	12¹/₄

Children's Intarsia Sweater

TENSION

20 sts and 30 rows measured over 10cm (approx 4 in) of St st and Intarsia pattern using 4.00mm needles.

BACK AND FRONT

Using 3.75mm needles and Col A, cast on 84(94) sts and work 12 rows in K2, P2 rib. Change to 4.00mm needles and St st, and work Intarsia pattern and shaping as per graph, leaving centre 10(12) sts of back and front neck on a st holder.

SLEEVES

Using 3.75mm needles and Col A, cast on 36(40) sts and work 12 rows in K2, P2 rib. Change to 4.00mm needles and working in St st, inc 1 st at each end of every 4th row 17(18) times [70(76) sts].
Work 4(6) rows without shaping [74(82) rows] or until length desired. Cast off.

MAKING UP

Press all pieces gently, except ribs, on WS using a warm iron over a damp cloth. With RS facing, join right shoulder seam, matching sts, using backstitch.
Neckband Using 3.75mm needles and Col A, pick up 16 sts down left side front neck, 10(12) sts on st holder, 16 sts along right front side and 32 sts across back neck [74(78) sts].
Work 12 rows in K2, P2 rib. Cast off.
Join neck and second shoulder seam.
Mark 47(52) rows from shoulder seam on each side. Centre sleeve and join to armhole between markers, matching 3 sts on sleeve top to 4 rows on armhole.
Join side and sleeve seams.

EMBROIDERY

Using french knots and chain st, embroider flowers as shown in photograph (page 68).

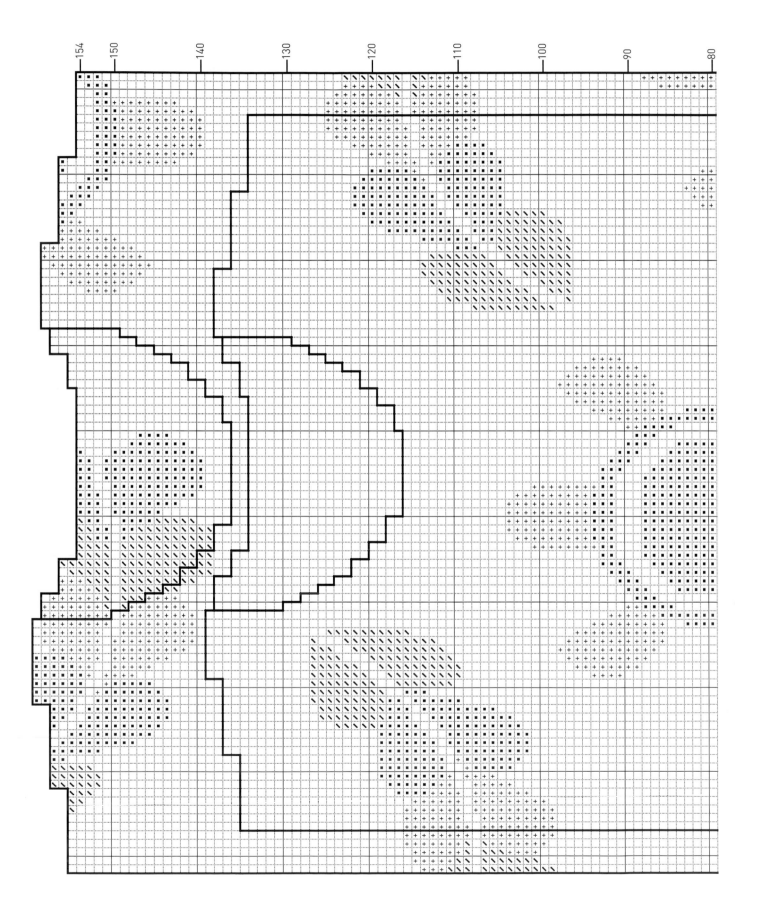

Looking casual yet dressed for the occasion wearing this elegant oyster cotton lace sweater.

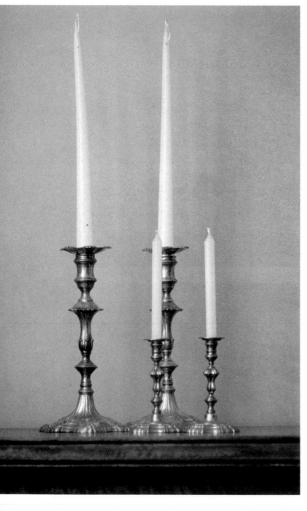

Above and opposite, **Lacy Sweater**, pattern on page 80.

a touch of luxury

Top and opposite, **Cotton Scarf**, pattern on page 81.
Bottom, **Lacy Sweater**, pattern on page 80.

Lacy Sweater

This feminine cotton sweater uses repeat lace patterning and is edged with Garter stitch on the bodice, cuffs and neckline.

Lacy Sweater

YARN

Colour	Quantity			
Size	A	B	C	D
Jo Sharp Soho Summer DK Cotton x 50g balls				
235 Oyster	8	9	10	11

NEEDLES

1 pair 3.75mm needles (USA 5) (UK 9).
1 pair 4.00mm needles (USA 6) (UK 8).
2 stitch holders.

MEASUREMENTS

Measurements given in inches are approximate.

Women's sizing	A	B	C	D
To fit bust				
cm	80	90	100	110
in	31½	35½	39½	43½
Bodice circumference				
cm	84	92	100	108
in	33	36¼	39½	42½
Bodice length				
cm	54	58	60	64
in	21¼	22¾	23½	25¼
Sleeve length (seam)				
cm	41	44	47	50
in	16¼	17¼	18½	19¾

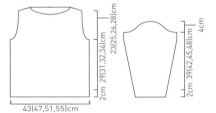

PATTERN

TENSION

22 sts and 26 rows measured over 10cm (approx 4 in) of Pattern Repeat using 4.00mm needles.

PATTERN REPEAT

Row 1 (WS) Purl.
Row 2 K3, * yo, K2, sl 1, K1, psso, K2tog, K2, yo, K1; rep from * to last st, K1.
Row 3 Purl.
Row 4: K2, * yo, K2, sl 1, K1, psso, K2tog, K2, yo, K1; rep from * to last 2 sts, K2.
Repeat these 4 rows.

BACK

Using 3.75mm needles, cast on 94(103,112, 121) sts. Knit 5 rows.
Change to 4.00mm needles. Beg with Row 1, work in patt rep until 19(20,21,22) patts have been completed.
Work Row 1 (WS) of next patt.
Shape armholes (RS) Keeping patt correct, cast off 4 sts at beg of this and next row.
Next row (RS) Dec 1 st at each end of this and foll alt rows 4 times [76(85,94,103) sts].
Cont in patt until 33(35,37,39) patt reps have been completed from the start [137(145,153,161) rows incl band].
Work Row 1 (WS) of next patt.
Shape back neck and shoulder
(RS) Keeping patt correct, cast off 6(7,9,10) sts, patt 22(25,28,31) sts, turn.
(WS) Cast off 5 sts, patt to end.
(RS) Cast off 6(7,9,10) sts, patt to end.
(WS) Cast off 5 sts, patt to end.
Cast off rem 6(8,9,11) sts.
With RS facing, leave 20(21,20,21) sts on a st holder.
Rejoin yarn to rem sts. Work second side to match first side, rev all shaping.

FRONT

Work as for back until 28(30,32,34) patt reps have beeen worked from the start [117(125,133,141) rows incl band].
Work Row 1 (WS) of next patt.

Shape neck (RS) Work 28(32,37,41) sts, turn, leave 48(53,57,62) sts on a st holder.
Work each side of neck separately.
(WS) Cast off 2 sts at beg (neck edge) of this row, then 1 st at neck edge of foll alt rows, 8 times [18(22,27,31) sts].
Shape shoulder (RS) Cast off 6(7,9,10) sts at beg of this and foll alt row.
Work 1 row. Cast off rem 6(8,9,11) sts.
With RS facing, leave 20(21,20,21) centre sts on a st holder. Join yarn to rem sts. Work second side to match first side, rev all shaping.

SLEEVES

Using 3.75mm needles, cast on 40(49,49,58) sts. Knit 5 rows.
Change to 4.00mm needles.
Working in patt rep, and keeping patt correct, AT THE SAME TIME, shape sleeve as follows; inc 1 st at each end of every 4th row, 20 times [80(89,89,98) sts]. Cont in patt without further shaping until sleeve (incl band) measures 41(44,47,50)cm ending on a WS row.
Shape sleeve top (RS) Keeping patt correct, cast off 4 sts at beg of this and next row.
(RS) Dec 1 st at each end of this and foll alt rows 4 times. Cast off rem 62(71,71,80) sts.

MAKING UP

Press all pieces gently, on WS, using a warm iron over a damp cloth.
Using backstitch and matching sts, join right shoulder seam.
Neckband With RS facing, pick up 19(18,19,18) sts down left side of neck, 20(21,20,21) sts from holder on front neck, 19(18,19,18) sts up right side of neck, 10 sts from right side of back neck, 20(21,20,21) sts from holder on back neck, and 10 sts on left side of back neck [98 sts].
Work 5 rows in Garter st. Cast off.
Using Backstitch, join second shoulder and neck seam. Centre sleeves and join.
Join side and sleeve seams.

Cotton Scarf

A generous cotton scarf using an easy two row repeat pattern creating a lacy vertical rib effect. Made in two pieces, joined at the centre.

Cotton Scarf version 1

Cotton Scarf version 2

YARN

Version 1

Colour	Quantity
Size	One size

Jo Sharp Soho Summer DK Cotton x 50g balls
234 Currant   6

Version 2

Colour	Quantity
Size	One size

Jo Sharp Soho Summer DK Cotton x 50g balls
228 Calico   6

NEEDLES

1 pair 4.00mm needles (USA 6) (UK 8).

MEASUREMENTS

Meaurements given in inches are approximate.

Length - 188cm (74¼ in).
Width - 20cm (8 in).

188cm   20cm

PATTERN

TENSION

25 sts and 29 rows measured over 10cm (approx 4 in) of Lace Pattern using 4.00mm needles.

LACE PATTERN

Multiple 13 + 2
(RS) K1 * sl 1, K1, psso, K3, yon, K3, yon, K3, K2tog; rep from * to last st, K1.
(WS) Knit.

SCARF

Using 4.00mm needles, cast on 54 sts.
Work in Lace Pattern until length measures 94cm. Cast off.
Make a second piece the same as the first.

MAKING UP

With RS facing, using Backstitch, join two pieces tog along cast off edges.

the satisfaction
of relaxing after
a successful day

Classic cable
combinations
add texture
and interest.

Above, **Chequered Cushions** versions 1 and 2, pattern on page 88, **Mohair Singlet** version 2, pattern on page 48. Above left, (from left to right) **Silkroad DK Tweed** in 416 Cocoa, 417 Fleece, 418 Iceberg. Opposite, **Cabled Cushion** version 1, pattern on page 102.

rich and sumptuous

Chequered Cushion

This cushion features a chequer pattern of cable and reverse Stocking stitch and a Garter stitch border.

Chequered Cushions versions 1 (left) and 2 (right)

YARN

Version 1

Colour	Quantity
Size	One size

Jo Sharp Classic DK Wool x 50g balls

347 Orient	5

Version 2

Colour	Quantity

Jo Sharp Classic DK Wool x 50g balls

301 Natural	5

NEEDLES

1 pair 4.00mm needles (USA 6) (UK 8).
1 cable needle.

FILLING

1 40cm x 40cm cushion insert.

MEASUREMENTS

Measurements given in inches are approximate.

Width - 40cm (15³/₄ in).
Length - 40cm (15³/₄ in)

```
            40cm
       ┌──────────┐
       │          │
       │ Cushion  │ 40cm
       │          │
       └──────────┘
            40cm
```

PATTERN

TENSION

22.5 sts and 30 rows measured over 10cm (approx 4 in) of Cable Pattern using 4.00mm needles.

SPECIAL ABBREVIATIONS

Cross 2 R - slip 2 sts onto a cable needle and hold at back of work, K next 2 sts, then K the 2 sts from cable needle.

Cross 2 L - slip 2 sts onto a cable needle and hold at front of work, K next 2 sts, then K the 2 sts from cable needle.

CABLE PATTERN

(24 sts)

Rows 1, 3, 5 & 7 *K12, P12.
Row 2 and alt rows *K the P sts and P the K sts of previous row.
Row 9 *Cross 2 R, K4, Cross 2 L, P12.
Rows 11, 13, 15 & 17 *K12, P12.
Rows 19, 21, 23 & 25 *P12, K12.
Row 27 *P12, Cross 2 R, K4, Cross 2 L.
Rows 29, 31, 33 & 35 *P12, K12.
Row 36 As row 2.
These 36 rows form pattern repeat.

CUSHIONS

(Make 2)

Using 4.00mm needles, cast on 84 sts.
Knit 8 rows (Garter st).
Next row (RS) K6, work row 1 of cable patt, rep from * 3 times, K6.
(WS) K6, work row 2 of patt rep to last 6 sts, K6.
These 2 rows set patt. Cont working in cable patt as set for 36 rows. Repeat these 36 rows, twice more. Knit 8 rows. Cast off.

MAKING UP

Press pieces gently on WS using a warm iron over a damp cloth. Using backstitch, join on 3 sides. Position cushion insert and sew remaining side.

Button Cushion

This round striped cotton cushion cover is started at the centre and worked outwards with gradual increases. The back piece is knitted in one colour and a button is attached through the centre, forming a dimple.

Button Cushion

YARN

Colour	Quantity
Size	One size

Jo Sharp Soho Summer DK Cotton x 50g balls

Col A	233 Crete	3
Col B	224 Thyme	1
Col C	235 Oyster	1
Col D	228 Calico	1

NEEDLES

1 long pair 4.00mm needles (USA 6) (UK8).

FILLING & BUTTONS

40cm round cushion insert.
2 x 2cm buttons.

MEASUREMENTS

Measurements given in inches are approximate.

Diameter - Approx 40cm (15³/₄ in).

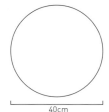

40cm

PATTERN

TENSION

22.5 sts and 30 rows measured over 10cm (approx 4 in) of St st using 4.00mm needles.

BACK

Using Col A, cast on 14 sts.
Row 1 (RS) K1, inc into each of next 12 sts, K1 [26 sts].
Rows 2, 4, 6, 8 (WS) Purl.
Row 3 (RS) K2,* M1, K2, rep from * to end of row [38 sts].
Row 5 (RS) K1, *M1, K3, rep from * to last st, K1 [50 sts].
Row 7 (RS) Work as row 5 [66 sts].
Row 9 (RS) K1, * M1, K4, rep from* to last st, K1 [82 sts].
This row sets the pattern of increases, which are now worked on every 4th row (which will be a RS row).
Add 1 extra st after each M1, as follows
Row 13 (RS) K1, *M1, K5, rep from * to last st, K1 [98 sts].
Row 17 (RS) K1, *M1, K6, rep from * to last st, K1 [114 sts].
Cont incs until there are 16 sts after each M1 [274 sts, 57 rows]. Work 3 rows [60 rows].
Cast off, leaving long end for seam.

FRONT

Work front as for back in colour sequence as follows:
Start with Colour D.
*Col D, 2 rows,
Col C, 4 rows,
Col D, 2 rows,
Col A, 4 rows,
Col B, 2 rows,
Col C, 6 rows,
Col D, 2 rows,
Col A, 2 rows,
Col B, 4 rows,
Rep from *,
Col C, 4 rows [60 rows].
Cast off leaving long end for seam.

MAKING UP

Join seam from centre to edge, with RS facing. To make an invisible seam, use Backstitch, matching row to row and positioning the seam between the first 2 sts on each edge.
Take the thread through all the cast on sts and pull them into a tight ring. Stitch firmly on WS.
With RS facing, join outside edges using backstitch, leaving a 15cm gap.
Turn RS out, insert filling and finish edge seam. Sew buttons to centre on each side stitching all the way through the cushion, drawing tightly.

cute as a button

Above, **Children's Cabled Sweater**, pattern on page 92.
Opposite, **Button Cushion**, pattern on page 89.

Children's Cabled Sweater

A richly cabled sweater with drop shoulder shaping and ribbed edgings on bodice, collar and sleeves.

Children's Cabled Sweater

YARN

Colour	Quantity		
Size	3 - 4	5 - 6	7 - 8 yrs
Jo Sharp Classic DK Wool x 50g balls			
355 Paris	8	10	12

NEEDLES

1 pair 3.75mm needles (USA 5) (UK 9).
1 pair 4.00mm needles (USA 6) (UK 8).
1 3.75mm circular needle (USA 5) (UK 9).
2 stitch holders.
1 cable needle.

MEASUREMENTS

Measurements given in inches are approximate.

Children's sizing	3 - 4	5 - 6	7 - 8 yrs
To fit chest			
cm	57-61	62-66	67-71
in	22¹/₂-24	24¹/₂-26	26¹/₄-28
Bodice circumference			
cm	70	78	86
in	27¹/₂	30³/₄	34
Bodice length			
cm	36	40	44
in	14¹/₄	15³/₄	17¹/₄
Sleeve length			
cm	27	29	31
in	10¹/₂	11¹/₂	12¹/₄

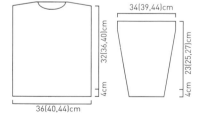

34(39,44)cm

32(36,40)cm

4cm

36(40,44)cm

23(25,27)cm

4cm

PATTERN

TENSION

20 sts and 32 rows measured over 10cm (approx 4 in) of Garter st using 4.00mm needles.

SPECIAL ABBREVIATIONS

T3B - Slip next st onto cable needle and hold at back of work, K next 2 sts from left hand needle, then P st from cable needle.

T3F - Slip next 2 sts onto cable needle and hold at front of work, P next st from left hand needle, then K sts from cable needle.

C6B or C6F - Slip next 3 sts onto cable needle and hold at back (or front) of work, K next 3 sts from left hand needle, then K sts from cable needle.

MB (make bobble) - (K1, P1) 3 times all into next st, pass 2nd, then 3rd, 4th, 5th and 6th sts over first st and off needle (bobble completed).

RT - Knit into front of 2nd st on needle, then K first st, slipping both sts off needle at the same time.

PANEL A (6 STS)

Row 1 Knit.
Row 2 Purl.
Row 3 C6B.
Row 4 Purl.
Rep these 4 rows.

PANEL B (15 STS)

Row 1 P5, K2, MB, K2, P5.
Row 2 K5, P5, K5.
Row 3 P5, MB, K3, MB, P5.
Row 4 K5, P5, K5.
Row 5 As row 1.
Row 6 As row 2.
Row 7 P4, T3B, P1, T3F, P4.
Row 8 K4, P2, K1, P1, K1, P2, K4.
Row 9 P3, T3B, K1, P1, K1, T3F, P3.
Row 10 K3, P3, K1, P1, K1, P3, K3.
Row 11 P2, T3B, (K1, P1) twice, T3F, P2.
Row 12 P4, K1, (P1, K1) 3 times, P4.
Row 13 K5, P1, (K1, P1) twice, K5.
Row 14 As row 12.

Row 15: K2, T3F, P1, (K1, P1) twice, T3B, K2.
Row 16: As row 10.
Row 17: P3, T3F, K1, P1, K1, T3B, P3.
Row 18: As row 8.
Row 19: P4, T3F, P1, T3B, P4.
Row 20: K5, P5, K5.
Rep these 20 rows.

PANEL C (14 STS)

Row 1 Knit.
Row 2 Purl.
Row 3 C6B, K2, C6F.
Row 4 Purl.
Rep these 4 rows.

PANEL D (6 STS)

Row 1 Knit.
Row 2 Purl.
Row 3 C6F.
Row 4 Purl.
Rep these 4 rows.

PANEL E (2 STS)

Row 1 RT.
Row 2 P2.
Rep these 2 rows.

BACK

Using 3.75mm needles, cast on 94(102,110) sts. Work 10 rows in K2, P2 rib. Change to 4.00mm needles and establish position of panels, starting at Row 1 of each panel.
Row 1 (RS) K10(12,14), Panel A, K3(4,5), Panel E, Panel B, Panel E, K3(4,5), Panel C, K3(4,5), Panel E, Panel B, K3(4,5), Panel D, K10(12,14). Cont as set, working in Garter st (K every row) on all K sts. Complete 100(114,128) rows from band (count on Garter st at edge).
Shape back neck and shoulders (RS) Cast off 9(10,11) sts at beg of row, then cont in patt until there are 28(30,32) sts on the needle. Turn and leave rem sts on st holder.
(WS) Cast off 5 sts, patt to end.
(RS) Cast off 9(10,11) sts at beg of row, patt to end.
(WS) Cast off 5 sts at beg of row, patt to end.
(RS) Cast off rem 9(10,11) sts.
Leave first 20(22,24) sts on holder. Join yarn

to rem sts, patt 1 row. Work second side to match first side rev all shaping.

FRONT

Work as for back to row 82(94,106).
Shape front neck and shoulders (RS) Patt 37(40,43) sts, turn.
(WS) Cast off 2 sts at beg of this row and then dec 1 st at beg of next 8 WS rows [27(30,33) sts].
Patt 0(2,4) more rows.
(RS) Cast off 9(10,11) sts at beg of this and next 2 RS rows.
Leave first 20(22,24) sts on st holder, patt 1 row. Work second side to match first side rev all shaping.

SLEEVES

Using 3.75mm needles, cast on 50(54,58) sts and work 10 rows in K2, P2 rib, inc 1 st at centre of last row (51(55,59) sts).
Change to 4.00mm needles and establish position of panels, starting at row 1 of each panel.
Row 1 (RS) K7(8,9), Panel A, K3(4,5), Panel E, Panel B, Panel E, K3(4,5), Panel D, K7(8,9).
Cont as set, working in Garter st (K every row) on all K sts, increasing at each end of every 4th row 12(15,18) times, [75(85,95) sts], then work without further shaping until 74(80,86) rows have been completed from band. Cast off.

MAKING UP

Press all pieces gently, on WS, using a warm iron over a damp cloth. Join shoulder seams Centre sleeves and join to armhole. Join side and sleeve seams.
Neckband With RS facing, using 3.75mm circular needle, pick up 10,(11,12) sts down left side front neck, 20(22,24) sts from st holder, 10(11,12) sts along right side front neck, 8(9,10) sts along right side back neck, 20(22,24) sts from st holder at centre back and 8(9,10) sts along left side back neck [76(84,92) sts].
Work 12 rounds K2, P2 rib. Cast off loosely and evenly in rib.

simple pleasures

Savour a
melting moment
with delicate
pastel shades.

Above right, **Women's Cabled Sweater**, pattern on page 98.
Above left, **Socks** version 2, pattern on page 99.

Above, **Chequered Cushions** versions 1 and 2, pattern on page 88.

Women's Cabled Sweater

This timeless classic sweater is worked with a neat flat diamond cable stitch and bands in 2 x 2 rib.

Women's Cabled Sweater

YARN

Colour	Quantity			
Size	A	B	C	D
Jo Sharp Classic DK Wool x 50g balls				
353 Fleur	16	17	18	19

NEEDLES

1 pair 4.00mm needles (USA 6) (UK 8).
1 4.00mm circular needle (USA 6) (UK 8).
1 cable needle.
2 stitch holders.

MEASUREMENTS

Measurements given in inches are approximate.

Women's sizing	A	B	C	D
To fit bust				
cm	80	90	100	110
in	31½	35½	39¼	43¼
Bodice circumference				
cm	94	105	116	128
in	37	41½	45¾	50½
Bodice length				
cm	65	68	71	74
in	25½	26¾	28	29
Sleeve length				
cm	45	47	48	50
in	17¾	18½	19	19¾

48(53.5,59,65)cm

42(42,46,46)cm

59(62,65,68)cm

6cm

41(43,44,46)cm

4cm

PATTERN

TENSION

27 sts and 27 rows measured over 10cm (approx 4 in) of Cable Pattern using 4.00mm needles.

SPECIAL ABBREVIATIONS

T2F (Twist 2 front) - slip next st onto cable needle and hold at front of work, purl next st from left hand needle, then knit st from cable needle.

T2B (Twist 2 back) - slip next st onto cable needle and hold at back of work, knit next st from left hand needle, then purl st from cable needle.

CABLE PATTERN

(15 sts)
Row 1 (RS) *P3, (T2B) twice, P1, (T2F) twice, P3; rep from *.
Row 2 *K3, (P1,K1,P1,K3) twice; rep from *.
Row 3 *P2, (T2B) twice, P3, (T2F) twice, P2; rep from *.
Row 4 *K2, P1, K1, P1, K5, P1, K1, P1, K2; rep from *.
Row 5 *P1, (T2B) twice, P5, (T2F) twice, P1; rep from *.
Row 6 *(K1, P1) twice, K7, (P1, K1) twice; rep from *.
Row 7 *(T2B) twice, P7, (T2F) twice; rep from *.
Row 8 *P1, K1, P1, K9, P1, K1, P1; rep from *.
Row 9 (T2F) twice, P7, (T2B) twice.
Row 10 As row 6.
Row 11 * P1, (T2F) twice, P5, (T2B) twice, P1; rep from *.
Row 12 As row 4.
Row 13 *P2, (T2F) twice, P3, (T2B) twice, P2; rep from *.
Row 14 As row 2.
Row 15 *P3, (T2F) twice, P1, (T2B) twice, P3; rep from *.
Row 16 *K4, (P1, K1) 3 times, P1, K4.
Rep these 16 rows.

BACK

Using 4.00mm needles, cast on 130(142,158,174) sts. Work 12 rows in K2, P2 rib, increasing 0(3,2,1) sts on last row [130(145,160,175) sts].
Establishment rows.
Row 1 (RS) P5, then 8(9,10,11) reps of cable row 1, P5.
Row 2 (WS) K5, then * 8(9,10,11) reps of cable row 2, P5.
These 2 rows set patt.
Cont working in patt until 10(10.5,11,11.5) patts have been completed [160,(168,176,184) rows excluding band].
Shape back neck and shoulders (RS) Cast off 10(12,14,15) sts, then patt 42(47,52,58) sts and leave rem sts on st holder.
(WS) Cast off 5 sts, patt to end.
(RS) Cast off 10(12,14,14) sts, patt to end.
(WS) Cast off 5 sts, patt to end.
(RS) Cast off 11(12,14,16) sts, patt to end.
(WS) Patt 1 row.
(RS) Cast off rem 11(13,14,16) sts.
With RS facing , leave 26(27,28,29) sts on a holder.
Rejoin yarn to rem sts.
Keeping patt correct, work 1 row on rem sts, then work secong side to match first side, rev all shaping.

FRONT

Work as for back to row 140(148,156,164) excluding band.
Shape front neck and shoulders (RS)
Work 52(59,66,73) sts. Turn, leaving rem sts on a holder.
(WS) Keeping patt correct, dec 1 st at beg (neck edge) of this row and next 9 (WS) rows [42(49,56,63) sts].
(RS) Cast off 10(12,14,15) sts at beg of this row.
Work 1 row.
(RS) Cast off 10(12,14,16) sts at beg of this row.
Work 1 row.
(RS) Cast off 11(12,14,16) sts at beg of this row.
Work 1 row.
Cast off rem 11(13,14,16) sts.
Leave 26(27,28,29) sts on holder, then keeping patt correct, work 1 row, then second side to match first side, rev all shaping

SLEEVES

Using 4.00mm needles, cast on 58(58,70,70) sts and work 8 rows in K2, P2 rib, inc 4(4,7,7) sts evenly across last row [62(62,77,77) sts].
(RS) P1, work 4(4,5,5) cable patt repeats starting at Row 1, P1.
Keeping patt correct, inc 1 st at each end of every 4th row 25(25,24,24) times [112(112,125,125) sts, 100(100,96,96) rows excluding band].
Cont without further shaping for 12(16,24,28) rows [112(116,120,124) rows] or until length desired. Cast off

MAKING UP

Press all pieces gently, except ribs, on WS, using a warm iron over a damp cloth.
With RS facing, using Backstitch join shoulders. Centre sleeves and join.
Join side and sleeve seams.
Neckband With RS facing, using 4.00mm circular needles, pick up 28 sts on left side front neck, 26(27,28,29) sts from holder on centre front neck, 28 sts up right side front neck, 10(9,10,9) sts down right side back neck, 26(27,28,29) from holder on centre back neck and 10(9,10,9)sts along left side back neck [128(128,132,132) sts. Work 20 rounds K2, P2 rib. Cast off in rib.

Socks

Cool cotton socks with fully shaped foot and ribbed ankle.

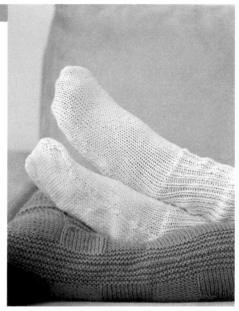

Socks version 1

Version 1

Colour	Quantity
Size	One size

Jo Sharp Soho Summer DK Cotton x 50g balls
228 Calico   3

Version 2

Colour	Quantity
Size	One size

Jo Sharp Soho Summer DK Cotton x 50g balls
233 Crete   3

NEEDLES

1 pair 4.00mm needles (USA 6) (UK 8).

MEASUREMENTS

Measurements given in inches are approximate. Average size given

17cm

20cm

PATTERN

TENSION

22.5 sts and 30 rows measured over 10cm (approx 4 in) of St st using 4.00mm needles.

SOCKS
(Make 2)

Using 4.00mm needles, cast on 25 sts and work 46 rows in K1, P1 rib.
Change to St st, and work 52 rows, ending on a WS row.
Shape toe Work in short rows, turning after stated number of sts, leaving rem sts at end of needle.
K23, P21, K19, P17, K15, P13.
Next row K all 19 sts on needle, including sts left at end of needle. Turn and P all 25 sts.
Turn, marking each end of this row.
K19, P13, K15, P17, K19, P21, K23, P25.
Cont in St st, work 36 rows.
Shape heel Work this shaping exactly as toe shaping. Cont in St st, work 12 rows, finishing on a WS row.
Now working in K1, P1 rib, work 46 rows.
Cast off in rib.

MAKING UP

With RS facing, fold at marker and using edge to edge st, join seams from toe to top of rib on each side.

Socks version 2

Wool, silk & cashmere
to cable, wrap and keep.

Above and opposite, **Tweed Throw**, pattern on page 103.
Mohair Singlet, pattern on page 48.

Cabled Cushion

Neat cables create a luxury look in this cushion. Separately knitted edging is sewn around the seams after finishing.

Cabled Cushion Version 1

Cabled Cushion Version 2

YARN

Version 1

Colour	Quantity
Size	One size

Jo Sharp Silkroad Aran Tweed x 50g balls
140 Goose   7

Version 2

Colour	Quantity
Size	One size

Jo Sharp Silkroad Aran Tweed x 50g balls
416 Cocoa   4

NEEDLES

Version 1
1 pair 5.00mm needles (USA 8) (UK 6).
Version 2
1 pair 4.00mm needles (USA 6) (UK 8).
Both versions
1 cable needle.

FILLING

Version 1
50cm cushion insert.
Version 2
40cm cushion insert.

MEASUREMENTS

Measurements given in inches are approximate.

Version 1
Width - 50cm (19³/₄ in)
Length - 50cm (19³/₄ in)

Version 2
Width - 40cm (15³/₄ in)
Length - 40cm (15³/₄ in)

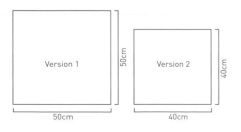

PATTERN

TENSION
Version 1
18 sts and 24 rows measured over 10cm (approx 4 in) of St st using 5.00mm needles.
Version 2
20 sts and 30 rows measured over 10cm (approx 4 in) of St st using 4.00mm needles.

SPECIAL ABBREVIATIONS
C12B - slip next 6 sts onto cable needle and hold at back of work, knit next 6 sts from left hand needle, then knit sts from cable needle.

CABLE PATTERN REPEAT
(18 sts + 4)
Row 1 (RS): K4, *P1, K12, P1, K4; rep from * 6 times.
Row 2: P4, *K1, P12, K1, P4; rep from * 6 times.
Rep these 2 rows, once more.
Row 5: K4,*P1, C12B, P1, K4; rep from * 6 times.
Row 6: P4,* K1, P12, K1, P4; rep from * 6 times.
Rep these 6 rows.

VERSION 1 FRONT & BACK
(Make 2)
Using 5.00mm needles, cast on 112 sts. Work in Cable Pattern Repeat until length measures 50cm. Cast off.

VERSION 2 FRONT & BACK
(Make 2)
Using 4.00mm needles, cast on 112 sts. Work in pattern repeat until length measures 40cm. Cast off.

MAKING UP
Sew front and back pieces together along 3 sides using backstitch. Insert cushion filling and sew final side.

PICOT EDGING
Cast on 5 sts, using needle size relevant to version being knitted.
*Cast off 4 sts, slip remaining st on right hand needle, cast on 4 sts; rep from * until length is sufficient for version being knitted. Sew into place along 4 sides of cushion.

Tweed Throw

Eight narrow panels of flat cabled fabric are sewn together to create a chequer-board effect in this lightly textured throw.

Tweed Throw

Size	One size
Colour	Quantity

Jo Sharp Silkroad Aran Tweed x 50g balls

Col A	139 Spring	4
Col B	138 Dove	4
Col C	142 Taffeta	6
Col D	120 Ash	4

NEEDLES

1 pair 5.00mm needles (USA 8) (UK 6).
1 cable needle.
1 5.00mm circular needle (long).

MEASUREMENTS

Measurements given in inches are approximate.

Width - 110cm (43¼ in).
Length - 135cm (53¼ in).

135cm

110cm

PATTERN

TENSION

18 sts and 24 rows measured over 10cm (approx 4 in) of Pattern using 5.00mm needles.

SPECIAL ABBREVIATIONS

Cross 2 R - slip 2 sts onto a cable needle and hold at back of work, K next 2 sts, then K the 2 sts from cable needle.
Cross 2 L - slip 2 sts onto a cable needle and hold at front of work, K next 2 sts, then K the 2 sts from cable needle.

THROW PATTERN

The throw is made from 8 panels (2 each of 4 kinds).
Each panel is 24 sts wide, uses 9 repeats of the 36 row cable pattern (324 rows), changing colour at each repeat following colour sequences given.
Make panel Using 5.00mm needles and referring to col sequence for first col in panel being knitted, cast on 24 sts.
Rows 1, 3, 5 & 7 K12, P12.
Row 2 and alt rows K the P sts and P the K sts of previous row.
Row 9 Cross 2 R, K4, Cross 2 L, P12.
Rows 11, 13, 15 & 17 K12, P12.
Rows 19, 21, 23 & 25 P12, K12.
Row 27 P12, Cross 2 R, K4, Cross 2 L.
Rows 29, 31, 33 & 35 P12, K12.
Row 36 As row 2.
These 36 rows form the pattern repeat.
Cont in 36 row patt rep, changing colours at the beg of each rep following colour sequences given below for panel being knitted (324 rows). Cast off.

COLOUR SEQUENCE

Panel 1 Colours; A, B, C, D, A, B, C, D, A.
Panel 2 Colours; B, C, D, A, B, C, D, A, B.
Panel 3 Colours; C, D, A, B, C, D, A, B, C.
Panel 4 Colours; D, A, B, C, D, A , B, C, D.

MAKING UP

Press all pieces gently on WS, using a warm iron over a damp cloth.
Using Edge to Edge st join panels in a sequence of 1, 2, 3, 4, 1, 2, 3, 4.

EDGE

With RS facing, using preferred col and a long 5.00mm circ needle to accommodate a large number of sts, pick up st for st along lower edge and work 10 rows in Garter st, inc 1 st at each end of every row. Cast off loosely and evenly. Repeat on top edge.
Pick up 3 sts to every 4 rows along left side and work as other edges, then rep on rem side. Join corner seams.

To achieve the best result with the least surprises, it is necessary to look carefully at the measurements given in a pattern and to do some simple homework before deciding which size garment to knit.

before you begin

After investing time and energy creating
a garment, avoid disappointment by
measuring twice and knitting once!

It is important to note that the ease allowed between body & garment circumference varies
from one design to the next, dependent upon the style intended by the designer, ie a garment
may be designed to fit snuggly or loosely.

The first step is to measure the chest/bust of the intended wearer. Next, compare this
measurement with the chest/bust measurements given in the pattern and choose the
appropriate size. Next, take a body length measurement from the base of the neck to the
desired finished sweater length and compare this to the measurement given in the pattern.

It may be necessary to make an alteration to the length. If the pattern given is worked to a
specified length by measurement as the work is in progress, then changing the length as the
work proceeds will be a simple matter. However if the pattern is worked to rows and
progressive length is not given, it may be a little more challenging. In this case, it will be
necessary to calculate the number of rows that are worked for each centimetre of length and
then to calculate the appropriate number of rows to be worked to achieve the length desired.

A reliable, alternative way to choose which size to knit is to use as a guide an existing favourite
old sweater that fits the intended wearer well. The sweater chosen for comparison should
preferably be of similar weight fabric and of similar cut, ie: drop shoulder or set in sleeve etc.
to the garment being knitted. Measure the width and length of the favourite old garment (as
shown right) and compare these measurements with those given in the size diagram of the
pattern. Choose the size which is the closest match to the desired outcome.

CHECK YOUR TENSION

At the start of each pattern,
the required tension is
given. Before beginning,
it is most important that
a tension square is knitted.
Incorrect tension will result
in mis-shaped pieces,
which may not fit together
or result in the wrong size.

HOW TO MEASURE TENSION
Using the yarn, needle size
and stitch pattern specified in
the pattern, cast on 40 sts
and work approximately 40
rows. Lay work flat and
without stretching, measure
10cm both vertically and
horizontally. Mark with pins.
Count the stitches and rows
between the pins, these
should match the required
tension. If not, try changing
up or down a needle size.

CHOOSING DIFFERENT NEEDLE SIZES
If your tension is too loose (too few stitches and rows),
try a smaller needle. If it is too tight (too many stitches
and rows) try a larger needle.

Note: Using a yarn other than that which is specified
in the pattern can produce unpredictable results.

Left, These swatches are knitted in the same yarn and
are the same number of stitches and rows, but with different
needle sizes.

basic techniques

These step by step instructions will get the beginner knitter
started on their first project.

STEP 1
Make a slip knot about 30cm
from end of yarn. Place slip knot
on a needle.
This creates the first stitch.

STEP 2
Insert right needle through loop
and wrap yarn under then over
right needle.

STEP 3
Use right needle to draw yarn
through first loop. This creates
the second stitch.

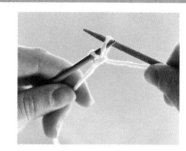

STEP 4
Place this second stitch onto
left needle.

STEP 5
Insert right needle between first
two stitches, wrap yarn under
then over right needle.

STEP 6
Using right needle, draw yarn
through between the stitches to
create another stitch. Place this
stitch onto left needle. Repeat
these steps until desired number
of stitches has been cast on.

STEP 1
Knit the first two stitches.

STEP 2
Insert the left needle into the first
stitch on the right needle.

STEP 3
Pull this stitch over the second
stitch.

STEP 4
Slide this stitch off the left
needle. Knit another stitch and
repeat from step two until all
stitches have been cast off and
there is only one stitch on the
right needle. Cut the yarn, leaving
a 15cm tail, thread through final
stitch and pull to tighten.

STEP 1
With the yarn at the back of the work, insert the right needle through the front of the first stitch on left needle from front to back.

STEP 2
Wrap yarn under then over right needle.

STEP 3
Draw yarn through stitch on left needle using right needle.

STEP 4
Slip the original stitch off the left needle to complete knit stitch.

PURL

STEP 1
With the yarn at the front of the work, insert the right needle through the front of the first stitch on left needle from back to front.

STEP 2
Wrap yarn over then under the right needle.

STEP 3
Using right needle, draw yarn through stitch towards back of work.

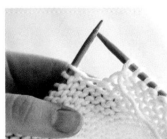

STEP 4
Slip original stitch off the left needle to complete purl stitch.

finishing your project

Using the correct technique to finish your garment will give it a professional look.

BACKSTITCH

Backstitch creates a strong and flexible seam, and is best used to join shoulders and armholes.

Note: This stitch is worked horizontally from right to left. Pieces can be pinned together before stitching if preferred.

STEP 1
Place right sides of garment together, aligning edges at top.

STEP 2
Secure yarn through both pieces at right hand edge, one row from the top.

STEP 3
Starting with needle at back of work, pull needle through to front one stitch to the left.

STEP 4
Move needle back one stitch to the right and insert through work, then back through two stitches to the left.

STEP 5
Repeat Step 4 until seam is completed.

EDGE TO EDGE STITCH

Also know as "Invisible Seam", Edge to Edge Stitch creates an invisible finish when used to join side and sleeve seams.

Note: This stitch is worked vertically from bottom to top.

STEP 1
Place the two pieces of work side by side with right sides facing. Secure yarn on wrong side of one piece at bottom edge.

STEP 2
Bring yarn through bottom edge at corner from back to front on the second piece.

STEP 3
Take needle over to the first piece, picking up the horizontal center bar of first stitch. Pull yarn through tightly to secure.

STEP 4
Take needle back to second piece and pick up horizontal bar of first stitch. Draw thread through, then back across horizontal bar of second row of first piece.
Repeat, matching rows until seam is completed.

Jo Sharp publications

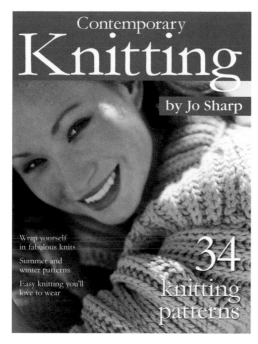

Contemporary Knitting

120 pages, soft cover.

34 designs, including easy to knit projects for beginners, and contemporary classics for men and women.

Features Jo Sharp Classic DK Wool, Silkroad and Rare Comfort Kid Mohair yarns.

Available from your local yarn store.
To find your nearest stockist, see 'where to shop' on pages 112 - 114, or visit www.josharp.com.au

Also available at selected newsagents, for details visit www.universalshop.com.au
or call 1300 303 414 (local call cost within Australia only) or +61 2 9887 0339 (International).

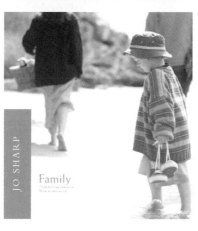

Jo Sharp knitting pattern books

Home, Gathering, Village and Family.

A series of stylish books containing an assortment of hand knitting patterns for the home and family.

These books are available from your local yarn store.
To find your nearest stockist, see 'where to shop' on pages 110 - 112 or visit www.josharp.com.au
or write to:
Jo Sharp
PO Box 1018
Fremantle 6959
Western Australia

Australia

WHOLESALE ENQUIRIES
Jo Sharp Hand Knitting Yarns
PO Box 1018,
Fremantle WA 6959

Ph: +61 8 9430 9699
Fax: +61 8 9430 9499

E: yarn@josharp.com.au
W: www.josharp.com.au

RETAIL STORES
AUSTRALIAN CAPITAL TERRITORY

Manuka	The Shearing Shed	02 6295 0061	www.theshearingshed.com.au
Mawson	Stitch 'n Time	02 6286 4378	

NEW SOUTH WALES

Beecroft	Knit It	02 9875 5844	www.knitit.com.au
Berrima	Berrima Patchwork & Craft	02 4877 1382	www.berrimapatchwork.com.au
Boolaroo	Pins & Things	02 4958 6362	
Bowral	Stepping Stones	02 4861 7077	
Byron Bay	Byron Bay Craft	02 6680 9951	
Dapto	Dapto Knit & Sew	02 4261 4633	
Guyra	Black Sheep Wool 'n' Wares	02 6779 1196	
Hornsby	Hornsby Wool & Craft Nook	02 9482 4924	
Katoomba	Katoomba Knit' & Needlcrft	02 4782 6137	
Lindfield	Greta's Handcraft Centre	02 9416 2489	
Merimbula	Pins & Needles	02 6495 3646	
Newcastle	Hand to Hand Crafts	02 4929 7255	
Newtown	Champion Textiles	02 9519 6677	
Orange	Fabulous Fringing	02 6360 0166	
Pennant Hills	Sue's Cherryhills	02 9484 0212	
Penrith	The Wool Inn	02 4732 2201	www.the-wool-inn.com.au
Port Macquarie	Port Macquarie Wool World	02 6583 7820	
Putney	Ozeyarn	02 9809 0895	www.ozeyarn.com
Sawtell	Sawtell Framing & Crafts	02 6658 2599	
Sydney	Tapestry Craft	02 9299 8588	www.tapestrycraft.com.au
Tamworth	Handy Hands	02 6766 6304	
Turramurra	Turramurra Drapery	02 9449 5843	
Wagga Wagga	Simply Stitches	02 69251767	
Yass	Sheep's Back Wool Gallery	0409 654 086	
Young	The Wool Room	02 6382 6665	www.thewoolroom.com.au

QUEENSLAND

Brisbane	Threads & More	07 3367 0864	www.threadsandmore.com.au
Cooroy	Cooroy Drapery	07 5447 6145	
Gympie	Craftnits	07 5482 6190	www.craftnits.com
Maleny	Maleny Wool Shop	07 5499 9052	
Tamborine Mountain	Ingrid's Crafts	07 5545 1196	

SOUTH AUSTRALIA

Firle	The Yarn Barn	08 8364 4866	
Glenelg	Barb's Sew & Knits	08 8294 7441	barbssewandknits.com.au
Highgate	Highgate Needle Nook	08 8271 4670	www.needlenook.com.au
Holden Hill	Needle Nook North East	08 8266 0518	
Mt Gambier	Stitch 'n' Knit	08 8725 5451	
Murray Bridge	Bridge Craftworld	08 8532 3799	
Woodside	Wildwood Arts & Crafts	08 8389 7500	

TASMANIA

Devonport	Needle 'n' Thread	03 6424 6920	
Hobart	Tasmanian Woollen Co	03 6234 1711	
Moonah	Tasmanian Wool Suppliers	03 6278 1800	
Sandy Bay	A Stitch In Time	03 6223 3871	

VICTORIA

Albert Park	Wool Baa	03 9690 6633	www.woolbaa.com.au
Bacchus Marsh	Bacchus Marsh Wool	03 5367 1514	
Brunswick East	The Knitter's Workshop	03 9383 7933	www.theknittersworkshop.com.au
Canterbury	Sunspun	03 9830 1609	www.sunspun.com.au
Castlemaine	Dorothy May's	03 5472 1043	
Dandenong	Wombat Wool	03 9774 8060	
Essendon	The Stitchery	03 9379 9790	www.stitchery.com.au
Highett	Lavender Cottage Cross Stitch	0416 179 813	
Kyabram	Kyabram Toyworld	03 5852 2862	
Malvern	Wondoflex	03 9822 8005	
Mansfield	Mansfield Craft Den	03 57752044	www.craftden.com.au
Melbourne	Wool Shop	03 9663 5088	
Melton	Melton Drapery	03 9743 5484	
Moorabbin	Wool Shop	03 9555 7344	
Mooroolbark	Mooroolbark Craft & Habby	03 9726 7291	www.mooroolbarkcraft.com.au
Mulgrave	Wool Village	03 9560 5869	
Olinda	Coach House Furniture Co.	03 9751 0161	
Omeo	Benambra Blue	03 5159 1248	
Prahran	AK Gallery	03 9533 7576	
Sunbury	Sunbury Wool & Craft	03 9744 4520	
Surrey Hills	Wool Shop	03 9836 9614	
Warrnambool	Uniform & Wool Centre	03 5562 9599	
Wendouree	Bits & Pieces Wool Shop	03 5339 5215	
West Rosebud	The Needley	03 5981 2641	
Williamstown	Stitchery Blue	03 9397 2005	

WESTERN AUSTRALIA

Albany	Boolah Art & Craft	08 9842 1042	
Claremont	Cotton Fields	08 9383 4410	
Cottesloe	Ivy & Maude	08 9383 3794	www.ivyandmaude.com
Innaloo	The Wool Shack	08 9446 6344	www.thewoolshack.com
Mt Pleasant	Cute 'n' Crafty	08 9315 3070	www.yarnsgalore.com.au
Subiaco	Crossways Wool & Fabrics	08 9381 4286	www.woolshop.com.au

New Zealand

RETAIL STORES

Knit World	
Christchurch	03 379 2300
Dunedin	03 477 0400
Henderson	09 837 6111
Hamilton	07 838 3868
New Plymouth	06 758 3171
Hastings	06 878 0090
Palmerston Nth	06 356 8974
Levin	06 367 9700
Tawa	04 232 8088
Lower Hutt	04 566 4689
Wellington	04 385 1918

MAIL ORDER
Knit World
PO Box 30645, Lower Hutt

Ph: +64 4 586 4530
Fax: +64 4 586 4531
Orders Only 0800 564884

E: knitting@xtra.co.nz
W: www.knitting.co.nz

USA

WHOLESALE ENQUIRIES
JCA Distribution
35 Scales Lane, Townsend MA 01469-1094
Phone: (978) 597-8794

RETAIL STORES
ALABAMA

Harvest	Little Barn	(800)542-3275	

ALASKA

Anchorage	Far North Yarn Co.	(907)299-0459	
Cordova	Net Loft	(907)424-7337	
Palmer	Fantastic Fibers	(907)745-7295	
Valdez	A Stitch Above	(907)299-0459	

ARIZONA

Mesa	Fiber Factory	(480)969-4346	www.fiberfactory.com
Prescott	Fiber Shop	(928)445-2185	
Sedona	Red Rock Knit Shop	(928)204-1505	
Surprise	Needlers Nest, Llc	(623)583-4411	
Tucson	Backdoor Bead	(520)745-9080	
Tucson	Purls	(520)797-8118	

ARKANSAS

Fayetteville	Hand Held		
Fayetteville	Spinning Star Fabrics	(479)443-2243	www.spinningstarfabrics.com
Little Rock	Handworks Gallery	(501)664-6300	www.handworksgallery.com

CALIFORNIA

Alpine	Lori's Frames	(619)659-9784	
Anaheim Hills	Velona Needlecraft	(800)972-1570	www.velona.com
Benicia	Benicia Knitting Circle	(707)746-5800	
Capitola	Yarn Place	(831)476-6480	www.theyarnplace.com
Carmel	Knitting By The Sea	(831)624-3189	
Davis	Sheep's Clothing	(530)759-9276	
El Cerrito	Skein Lane	(510)525-1828	www.skeinlane.com
Encinitas	Black Sheep	(760)436-9973	
Fort Bragg	Navarro River Knits	(877)468-9276	www.navarroriverknits.com
Fresno	Ancient Pathways	(559)264-1874	www.ancientpathways.net
Fresno	Janna's Needle Art	(559)227-6333	
Half Moon Bay	Fengari	(650)726-2550	www.fengari.com
La Mesa	Two Sisters and Ewe	(619)460-8103	
Lafayette	Yarn Boutique	(925)283-7377	www.yarnboutique.com
Long Beach	Liscat	(562)433-1733	
Los Altos	Uncommon Threads	(650)941-1815	
Los Angeles	Bea's Knit Shop	(310)474-0605	
Los Angeles	Knit Cafe	(323)658-5648	
Mendocino	Mendocino Yarn Shop	(888)530-1400	
Menlo Park	The Knitter's Studio	(650)322-9200	www.knittersstudio.com
Newbury Park	Weaver's Needle 'N Frame	(805)499-7979	
Newhall	Beads 'N Other Needs	(661)799-9595	
Oakland	Knitting Basket	(510)339-6295	www.theknittingbasket.com
Orinda	Infiknit Possibilities	(925)254-0933	
Palm Desert	Harriet's Yarn	(760)772-3333	
Redondo Beach	L'atelier	(310)540-4440	www.latelier.com
Riverside	Designer Handknits	(951)275-9711	
Rocklin	Filati Fine Yarns	(916)415-9430	www.filatiyarn.com
Rohnert Park	Elf Hand Knitwerks	(707)584-8635	www.sonic.net/jujubee
San Francisco	Atelier	(415)771-1550	
San Francisco	Greenwich Yarn	(415)567-2535	
San Francisco	Imagiknit	(415)621-6642	www.imagiknit.com
San Marino	A Stitch In Time	(626)793-5217	
San Rafael	Dharma Trading	(415)456-1211	www.dharmatrading.com
Santa Barbara	BB's Knits	(805)569-0531	
Santa Monica	Wildfiber	(310)458-2748	www.wildfiber.com
Santa Rosa	Caila Handknits	(707)545-4497	
Saratoga	Braid Box/Knitting Arts	(408)867-5010	
Sherman Oaks	Needle World	(818)784-2442	
Sonora	By Hand Gallery	(888)779-2767	www.www.byhandyarn.com
St Helena	Gail Laurence Studio	(707)967-9500	
Studio City	La Knitterie Parisienne	(818)766-1515	www.laknitterieparisienne.net
Thousand Oaks	Eva's Needlework	(805)379-0722	www.evasneedlework.com
Valley Village	Stitch Cafe	(818)980-1936	

COLORADO

Aspen	Yarn Gallery	(970)925-5667	
Colorado Springs	Needleworks by Holly Berry	(719)636-2752	
Denver	Ewenique Yarns	(303)377-6336	
Denver	Strawberry Tree	(303)759-4244	
Golden	Recycled Lamb	(303)234-9337	www.recycledlamb.com

United Kingdom

WHOLESALE ENQUIRIES
Viridian G & G Ltd
Unit 2B Barton Hill Trading Estate
Herapath Street
Barton Hill
Bristol BS5 9RD
UK

Ph: 0044 11 7941 2111
W: www.viridianyarns.co.uk

USA continued . . .

Grand Junction	Yarn Store	(970)241-5080	
Lakewood	Showers of Flowers	(303)233-2525	www.showersofflowers.com
Littleton	A Knitted Peace	(303)730-0366	www.aknittedpeace.com
Longmont	Natures Own Imagination	(303)530-5049	
Longmont	Theknitter.com	(866)402-5045	www.theknitter.com
Palisade	Cozy Knit & Purl	(970)464-1088	
Vail	Yarn Studio	(970)949-7089	

CONNECTICUT

Avon	Wool Connection	(860)678-1710	www.woolconnection.com
Deep River	Yarns Down Under	(860)526-9986	www.yarnsdownunder.com
East Haddam	Old Lyme Village Quilts	(860)434-2602	
Glastonbury	Village Wool	(860)633-0898	
Granby	Marji's Yarncrafts	(860)653-9700	
Greenwich	Knitting Niche	(203)869-6205	www.knittingniche.com
Mystic	Mystic River Yarns	(860)536-4305	
N. Branford	Yarns, Yarns, Yarns	(203)488-7370	
Stamford	Knit Together	(203)324-2500	www.knittogether.com
Stratford	Janet Kemp	(203)386-9276	
Vernon	Needle Arts Gallery	(860)871-1817	
Wallingford	Country Yarns	(203)269-6662	www.countryarns.com
Woodbridge	The Yarn Barn	(203)389-5117	www.theyarnbarn.com

DELAWARE

Bethany Beach	Sea Needles	(302)539-0574	www.seaneedles.com
Wilmington	Stitches With Style	(302)994-4329	

FLORIDA

Dunedin	Dunedin Needlepoint	(727)736-5392	
Jacksonville	A Stitch in Time	(904)731-4082	www.astitchintime.com
Largo	Ctr For Creative Expression	(727)593-3363	
Mount Dora	Knit 'N' Needle Nook	(352)383-4811	
Pensacola	King's Sewing & Knitting	(850)476-2660	
Port Charlotte	Creative Peddlar Crafts	(941)627-4658	
Sarasota	Knit Nook	(941)922-4233	
Winter Haven	Yarn Basket	(863)324-3665	

GEORGIA

Bogart	The Cat's Meow	(706)316-2130	
Dahlonega	Magical Threads Quilts & Bears	(706)867-8918	www.magicalthreads.com
Gainesville	Quilted Hearts	(770)536-3959	
Macon	Me And Thee	(478)474-6733	
Roswell	Cast-on Cottage	(770)998-3483	www.castoncottage.com

IDAHO

Boise	Drop A Stitch	(208)331-3767	
Ketchum	Isabel's Needlepoint	(208)725-0408	www.isabelspocket.com
Mccall	Keep Me In Stitches	(208)634-2906	
Meridian	Lisa's Yarn Shoppe	(208)884-4885	

ILLINOIS

Barrington	Gene Ann's Yarns & Gifts	(847)842-9321	www.geneannsyarns.com
Bloomington	Fiber Shop	(888)891-3002	www.fibershop.com
Champaign	Needleworks	(217)352-1340	www.cu-needleworks.com
Chicago	Arcadia Knitting	(773)293-1211	www.arcadiaknitting.com
Chicago	Nina	(773)486-8996	
Chicago	The Knitting Workshop	(773)929-5776	
Crystal Lake	Sunflower Samplings	(815)455-2919	
Des Plaines	Mosaic Yarn Studio Ltd.	(847)390-1013	
Glenview	Village Knit Whiz	(847)998-9772	
Northbrook	Three Bags Full	(847)291-9933	
Oak Park	Tangled Web Fibers	(708)445-8335	
Springfield	Nancy's Knitworks	(800)676-9813	
St. Charles	Wool and Company	(630)377-7033	www.woolandcompany.com
St. Charles	Fine Line	(630)584-9443	

INDIANA

Fort Wayne	Cass Street Depot	(260)420-2277	www.cassstreetdepot.com
Indianapolis	Mass Ave Knit Shop	(317)638-1833	
Valparaiso	Sheep's Clothing	(219)462-1700	
Westfield	Stitches & Scones	(317)896-4411	www.stitchesnscones.com

KANSAS

Manhatten	Wildflower Yarns	(785)537-1826	www.wildflowerknits.com
Olathe	Knit - Wit	(913)780-5648	
Wichita	Knits Etcetera	(316)652-0073	www.knitsetc.com
Wichita	Needleworks of Kansas	(316)871-7973	

KENTUCKY

Lexington	Knit One - Purl One	(859)268-0894	
Louisville	Sophie's Fine Yarn Shop	(502)254-5668	
Shelbyville	Handknitters	(502)254-9276	www.handknittersltd.com

LOUISIANA

New Orleans	Garden District	(504)453-9301	

MAINE

Auburn	Quiltessentials	(207)784-4486	
Bangor	City Side Yarn Company	(207)990-1455	
Camden	Unique One	(888)691-8358	www.uniqueone.com
Cape Elizabeth	Stitching Mantis	(207)767-5076	
Damariscotta	Pine Tree Yarns	(207)563-8909	www.lincoln.midcoast.com/elaine
Hallowell	Water Street Yarns	(207)622-5500	
Hancock	Shirleys Yarns & Crafts	(207)667-7158	
Kennebunk	Custom Shop	(207)985-3759	
Scarborough	Ardith Keef Yarn Shoppe	(207)883-8689	www.ardithkeef.com
Standish	Korner Knitters	(207)642-2894	www.kornerknitters.com

MARYLAND

Annapolis	Yarn Garden	(410)224-2033	www.yarngarden.com
Ashton	Fiber Works	(301)774-9031	
Baltimore	A Good Yarn	(410)327-3884	
Baltimore	Woolworks	(410)337-9030	
Bel Air	Ewenique Yarns	(410)399-9929	www.eweniqueyarns.com
Bethesda	Knit and Stitch Bliss	(301)652-8688	www.knitandstitch.com
Chesapeake City	Vulcan's Rest Fibers	(410)885-2890	
Columbia	All About Yarn	(410)992-5648	
Easton	Yarns & Co	(410)770-9388	
Fredrick	Keep Me In Stitches	(240)379-7740	www.keep-me-in-stitches.com
Glyndon	Woolstock	(410)517-1020	www.www.woolstock.com
Perryville	Ye Old Yarn Shop	(410)642-9896	
Rockville	Royal Yarns	(202)215-2300	www.royalyarns.com
Rockville	Wool Winders	(240)632-9276	www.woolwinders.com

MASSACHUSETTS

Amherst	Creative Needle	(413)549-6106	
Beverly	Abbott Yarn Shoppe	(978)927-1893	
Boston	Mary Jo Cole Needlework	(617)536-9338	
Brookfield	Knit Witts	(508)867-9449	www.knitwitts.com
Brookline	A Good Yarn	(617)731-4900	www.agoodyarnonline.com
Cambridge	Woolcott	(617)547-2837	
Cohasset	Creative Stitch	(781)383-0667	
Concord	Needle Arts Of Concord	(978)371-0424	www.needle-arts.com
Dennis	Ladybug Knitting Shop	(508)385-2662	www.ladybugknitting.com
Framingham	Fabric Place	(508)766-2194	www.fabricplace.com
Franklin	Mayflower Textiles	(508)528-3300	www.franklinmillstore.com
Harvard	Fiber Loft	(978)456-8669	
Ipswich	Loom 'N' Shuttle	(978)356-5551	
Lenox	Colorful Stitches	(413)637-8206	www.colorful-stitches.com
Lexington	Wild & Woolly Studio	(781)861-7717	
Littleton	World Stitches	(978)486-8330	
Milford	Knitting Pointers	(508)634-0099	
Milton	Snow Goose	(617)698-1190	
Needham	Black Sheep Knitting Co	(781)444-0694	
Needham	Creative Warehouse	(781)444-9341	
New Bedford	Hair Affair	(508)997-6677	
Northampton	Northampton Wools	(413)586-4331	
Northampton	Webs	(413)584-2225	www.yarn.com
Osterville	Knit Happens	(508)428-3882	
So. Hamilton	Cranberry Quillers	(978)468-3871	
So. Weymouth	Wooly Wooly Knit Shop		
Sturbridge	Mt Laurel Yarn Boutique	(508)347-0130	
Uxbridge	Knitting Garden	(508)278-2252	www.theknittinggarden.com
Walpole	Dees Nimble Needle	(508)668-8499	
Westboro	Necessities for Needlework	(508)366-1132	
Weston	Stitches The Threaded Needle	(781)891-4402	
Worcester	Knitters Paradise	(508)756-3000	
Worcester	Knit Latte	(508)754-6300	

MICHIGAN

Ann Arbor	Busy Hands	(734)996-8020	
Ann Arbor	Knit A Round Yarn Shop	(734)998-3771	
Beulah	Yarn Market	(231)882-4640	
Birmingham	Knitting Room	(248)540-3623	www.knittingroom.com
Birmingham	Right Off The Sheep	(248)646-7595	
Bloomfield	Melross	(248)258-9226	
Cedar	Irish Knits	(231)228-2800	
Davison	Elaine's Yarns	(810)653-9010	
Frankenmuth	Rapunzel's	(989)652-0464	www.zehnders.com
Fremont	Baa Baa Lamb Enchanted Ewe	(231)652-5262	
Grand Haven	Fibre House	(616)844-2497	www.forknitters.com
Grand Rapids	Threadbender Yarn Shop	(616)531-6641	www.threadbender.com
Holland	Friends of Wool	(616)395-9665	
Hudsonville	Whippletree Yarn & Gifts	(616)669-4487	
Jackson	Dropped Stitch	(517)758-8280	
Lake Orion	Heritage Spinning & Weaving	(248)693-3690	www.heritagespinning.com
Lansing	Threadbear	(517)703-9276	
Lathrup Village	Yarns And	(248)423-9200	
Macomb	Crafty Lady	(586)566-8008	
Marquette	Town Folk Gallery	(906)225-9010	www.townfolkgallery.com
Menominee	Elegant Ewe	(906)863-2296	
Okemos	Yarn For Ewe	(517)349-9665	
Plymouth	Old Village Yarn Shop	(734)451-0580	
Portage	Stitching Memories Inc.	(269)552-9276	
Tawas City	Tawas Bay Yarn Shop	(989)362-4463	
Traverse City	Baa Baa Blacksheep	(231)947-3160	
Traverse City	Lost Art	(231)941-1263	
Traverse City	Yarn Quest	(231)929-4277	
West Bloomfield	Rochelle Imber's	(248)855-2114	www.knitknitknit.com
West Branch	Evergreen Sampler	(989)345-1800	www.evergreensampler.com

MINNESOTA

Ely	Sisu Designs	(218)365-6613	
Knife River	Playing With Yarn	(218)834-5967	www.playingwithyarn.com
Minneapolis	Creative Fibers	(612)927-8307	www.creativefibers.com
Minneapolis	Depth of Field	(612)340-0529	www.depthoffieldyarn.com
Minneapolis	Linden Hills Yarns	(612)929-1255	
Minneapolis	Needlework Unlimited	(612)925-2454	www.needleworkunlimited.com
Minnetonka	Skeins	(952)939-4166	
Northfield	Cottage Industry	(507)664-3870	www.cottageindustry.net
Rochester	Just A Little Something	(507)288-7172	
Rochester	Kristen's Knits	(507)282-9501	
St. Paul	Three Kitten Yarn Shoppe	(651)457-4969	
St. Paul	Yarnery	(651)222-5793	
White Bear Lake	Sheepy Yarn Shoppe	(651)426-5463	www.sheepyyarnmn.com

MONTANA

Columbia	Hillcreek Fiber Studio	(573)449-5648	www.hillcreekfiberstudio.com
Columbia	Stitches	(573)446-3707	
Hamilton	Yarn Center	(406)363-1400	
Independence	Knitcraft Yarn Shop	(816)461-1248	www.knitcraft.com
Kansas City	The Studio	(816)531-4466	
Missoula	Joseph's Coat	(406)549-1419	
Missoula	Kaye's Creative Knitting	(406)721-5223	
Rolla	Uniquely Yours	(573)364-2070	
Springfield	Thread Peddler	(417)886-5404	
St. Louis	HearthStone Knits	(314)849-9276	
Stevensville	Wild West Wools	(406)777-4114	www.wild-west-wools.com

NEBRASKA

Omaha	Mangelsens	(402)391-4659	
Omaha	Personal Threads Boutique	(402)391-7733	www.personalthreads.com
Omaha	String Of Purls	(402)393-5648	

NEW HAMPSHIRE

Concord	Elegant Ewe	(603)226-0066	
Exeter	Chartottes Web	(603)778-1417	www.charlotteswebyarns.com
Meredith	Keepsake Quilting Inc	(603)253-8148	www.patternworks.com
Wilton	The Woolery	(603)654-7030	www.nhwoolery.com

NEW JERSEY

Belmar	Needles N Things	(732)681-6363	
Brigantine	Little Knit Shop	(609)266-9500	

USA continued . . .

Chatham	The Stitching Bee	(973)635-2691	
Colts Neck	Knitting Gallery	(732)294-9276	www.knittinggallery.com
Denville	Knitting Basket	(973)983-5648	
Garwood	Knitter's Workshop	(908)789-1333	
Lambertville	Simply Knit	(609)397-7101	www.simplyknit.com
Maplewood	Knit and Stitch	(973)761-8585	
Medford	Knitting Room	(609)654-9003	
Metuchen	Brass Lantern	(732)548-5442	
Mt. Holly	Woolbearers	(609)914-0003	
Ocean City	Seaside Knitting	(609)624-2410	
Princeton	Pins and Needles	(609)921-9075	
Riverdale	Knitter's Euphorium	(973)838-9942	
Sparta	Yarn Loft	(973)383-6667	

NEW MEXICO

Albuquerque	Village Wools	(505)883-2919	www.villagewools.com
Santa Fe	Needle's Eye	(505)982-0706	

NEW YORK

Bayside	Knit Wits	(718)229-0156	
Bedford Hills	Lee's Yarn Center	(914)244-3400	www.leesyarn.com
Bemus Point	Front Porch	(716)386-2524	
Brooklyn	Knitting Hands	(718)858-5648	
Buffalo	Elmwood Yarn Shop	(716)834-7580	www.elmwoodyarnshop.com
Chatham	Warm Ewe	(518)392-2929	
Coldspring	Knittingsmith	(845)265-6566	
Commack	Wild & Woolly Wools	(631)462-0391	
Cuddebackville	Bonnie's Kozy Knits	(845)754-0700	
Dewitt	The Village Yarn Shop	(315)449-2051	
Dix Hills	NewYork Knits	(585)924-1950	www.newyorkknits.com
East Aurora	Woolly Lamb	(716)655-1911	
Endicott	Cornucopia	(607)748-3860	
Garden City	Garden City Stitches	(516)739-5648	www.gardencitystitches.com
Geneva	Yarn Shop of Geneva	(315)789-7211	
Greenwich	Needleworks	(518)692-8980	
Huntington	The Knitting Corner	(631)421-2660	
New Hartford	Diana's Yarns & Crafts	(315)266-0005	
New York	Gotta Knit	(212)989-3030	
New York	Knitting 321	(212)772-2020	
New York	Lion & Lamb	(212)876-4303	
New York	Purl	(212)420-8796	
New York	Seaport Yarns	(212)608-3100	
New York	Woolgathering		
New York	Yarn Connection	(212)684-5099	
Nyack	Knitting Nation	(845)348-0100	
Oswego	North Wind Yarns	(315)349-9276	www.NorthWindYarns.com
Pawling	Yarn & Craft Box	(845)855-1632	
Port Washington	Knitting Place	(516)944-9276	
Remsen	Wool Haven	(315)794-3769	
Rochester	Village Yarn Shop	(585)454-6064	
Rockville Center	Knit N Tell	(516)678-7773	
Saratoga Springs	Saratoga Needle Arts	(518)583-2583	
Skaneateles	Elegant Needles	(315)685-9276	
Smithtown	Keep Me In Stitches	(631)724-8111	www.keepmeinstitches1.com
Troy	Lansingburgh Yarn Depot	(518)233-1052	
Wantagh	Knit Knacks	(516)785-2282	
West Sand Lake	Wool 'n Word	(518)674-5096	
White Plains	Yarns & Notions	(914)328-5706	
Williamsville	Karma Knitting	(716)631-9276	

NORTH CAROLINA

Raleigh	Great Yarns Inc	(919)832-3599	www.great-yarns.com
Southern Pines	Courtyard Shop	(910)692-8132	
Wilmington	Edge of Urge	(910)762-1662	

OHIO

Cincinnati	Knit Happens	(513)871-9276	
Columbus	Wolfe Fiber Arts	(614)487-9980	www.wolfefiberarts.com
Delaware	Stitch Stops Here	(740)362-9113	
Mansfield	Bumblebee Yarns	(419)525-1110	
Mt.Vernon	Craftsman Hill Fibers	(740)392-7724	www.craftsmanhill.com
Rocky River	River Color Studios	(440)333-9276	
Vermilion	Love To Knit Yarn Shop	(440)967-4073	

OKLAHOMA

Guthrie	Sealed With A Kiss	(405)282-8649	www.swakknit.com
Tulsa	Naturally Needlepoint	(918)747-8838	
Tulsa	StitchWorks	(918)496-3389	

OREGON

Ashland	Websters	(541)482-9801	www.yarnatwebsters.com
Bend	Juniper Fiberworks	(541)318-0726	
Cannon Beach	Siren Song Stitchery	(503)436-1300	
Carlton	Woodland Woolworks	(503)852-7376	
Corvallis	Fiber Nooks & Crannys	(541)754-8637	www.fncyarn.com
Hillsboro	Kathy's Knit Korner	(503)648-8525	
Lake Oswego	Molehill Farm	(503)697-9554	
Portland	Northwest Wools	(503)244-5024	www.northwestwools.com
Portland	Yarn Garden	(503)239-7950	

PENNSYLVANIA

East Berlin	The Mannings	(717)624-2223	www.the-mannings.com
Gilbertsville	Yarnsmith	(610)323-1553	www.yarnsmith.com
Greensburg	Knit Wits	(724)836-6922	
Harrisburg	Knitters Dream	(717)599-7665	www.knittersdream.com
Haverford	Busy Body's	(610)649-9477	
Jamison	Forever Yarn	(215)491-7670	
Kennett Square	Wool Gathering	(610)444-8236	
Lancaster	Oh Susanna	(717)393-5146	
Lansdale	Lamb's Wool	(215)361-9899	www.thelambswool.com
Ligonier	Kathy's Kreations	(724)238-9320	
Monroeville	Bonnie Knits	(412)856-7033	www.bonnieknits.com
Nazareth	Kramer Yarn Shop	(610)759-1294	
New Hope	Gazebo Plus	(215)862-0740	www.gazeboplus.com
Philadelphia	Rosie's Yarn Cellar	(215)977-9276	www.rosiesyarncellar.com
Philadelphia	Rosenfeld Industries	(215)601-3344	
Philadelphia	Sophie's Yarn	(215)925-5648	
Pine Grove Mills	Stitch Your Art Out	(814)200-4151	

Pittsburgh	Pittsburgh Knit & Bead	(412)421-7522	
Rochester Mills	Autumn House Farm	(724)286-9596	www.autumnhousefarm.com
Sayre	Mary's Fabric & Craft Ctr	(570)888-2320	
Sewickley	Yarns Unlimited Of Sewickly	(412)741-8894	
Shiremans Town	Colonial Yarn Shop	(717)763-8016	
Skippack	Yarnings	(267)663-4320	
Southampton	Knit Together	(215)355-3531	
Tunkhannock	Endless Mountain Quiltworks	(570)836-7575	
Willow Street	Legacy Yarns	(717)464-7575	

RHODE ISLAND

Newport	Knitting Needles	(401)841-5648	
Tiverton	Sakonnet Purls	(401)624-9902	www.sakonnetpurls.com
Warren	Bella Yarns	(401)247-7243	

SOUTH CAROLINA

Lexington	The Needler	(803)359-3858	

TENNESSEE

Knoxville	Knit ' N Purl	(865)690-9983	
Memphis	Yarniverse	(888)699-9276	www.yarniverse.com
Memphis	Yarns to Go	(901)454-4118	

TEXAS

Austin	Hill Country Weavers	(512)707-7396	
Bedford	Simpatico Yarns	(817)285-6067	www.simpaticoyarns.com
Dallas	Needle's Eye	(505)982-0706	
Fort Worth	Cabbage Rose	(817)377-3993	www.cabbagerosequilting.com
Fort Worth	Jenningstreet Yarns	(817)723-9562	
Houston	Nancy's Knits	(713)661-9411	
Judson	Stitches 'N Stuff	(903)663-3840	
Keller	Keepin' U In Stitches	(817)431-1234	www.pages.prodigy.net/pilotie
Plano	Woolie Ewe	(972)424-3163	www.wooliewe.com
San Antonio	Yarn Barn of San Antonio	(210)826-3679	

UTAH

Ogden	Needlepoint Joint	(801)394-4355	www.needlepointjoint.com
Salt Lake City	The Black Sheep Wool Co.	(801)487-9378	
Salt Lake City	Wool Cabin	(801)466-1811	www.woolcabin.com

VIRGINIA

Alexandria	Springwater Fiber Workshop	(703)549-3634	
Blacksburg	Bonomos	(540)951-8102	
Burke	Yarn Barn of Burke	(703)978-2220	
Charlottesville	The Needle Lady	(434)296-4625	
Falls Church	Aylin's Woolgatherer	(703)573-1900	www.aylins-wool.com
Lynchburg	Suzanne's Knit Shoppee	(804)384-7114	www.suzannesknittingyarns.com
Manassas	Old Town Needlecraft	(703)330-1846	
Midlothian	Got Yarn	(804)594-0323	www.gotyarn.com
Midlothian	MMNI Inc	(804)594-0323	
Raphine	Orchardside Yarn Shop	(540)348-5220	www.oysyarnshop.com
Stanardsville	Carodan Farm Wool Shop	(800)985-7083	www.carodanfarm.com
Staunton	Knitting Corner	(540)886-8641	
Vienna	Uniquities	(703)242-0520	
Virginia Beach	Ewe Knit Kits & Yarn	(757)498-4590	
Virginia Beach	Hook and I	(757)463-8869	www.hookandi.com
Virginia Beach	Knitting Corner	(757)420-7547	
Warrenton	Yorkshire Dales Knitwear	(540)349-0300	

VERMONT

Brattleboro	Not Just Yarn	(802)257-1145	
Montpelier	The Knitting Studio	(802)229-2444	
Shelburne	Knitter's Laine	(802)985-3223	
So. Burlington	Courtyard Fiberarts	(802)863-8081	
Waitsfield	Suzanne's	(802)496-6722	
Williston	Northeast Fiber Arts Studio	(802)288-8081	
Woodstock	Whippletree Yarn Shop	(802)457-1325	

WASHINGTON

Anacortes	Ana Cross Stitch	(360)299-9010	www.anacrossstitch.com
Bainbridge Is.	Churchmouse Yarns & Teas	(206)780-2686	www.churchmouseyarns.com
Bellevue	Skeins! Ltd	(425)452-1248	
Everett	Great Yarns!	(425)252-8155	www.greatyarns.com
Gig Harbor	Vintage	(253)265-1235	
Olympia	Canvas Works	(360)352-4481	
Port Hadlock	Dinah's Yarn Shop	(360)385-5230	
Poulsbo	Amanda's Yarns	(360)779-3666	
Poulsbo	Wild & Wooly	(360)779-3222	
Renton	Nancy's Knits	(425)255-7392	
Seattle	Acorn Street Shop	(206)525-1726	www.acornstreet.com
Seattle	FruFru.Biz	(206)329-8331	
Seattle	Full Circle	(206)783-3322	
Seattle	Hilltop Yarn Needlepoint	(206)283-8876	
Seattle	Pacific Fabrics & Crafts	(206)628-6222	
Seattle	Seattle Yarn Gallery	(206)935-2010	
Seattle	Tricoter	(206)328-6505	www.tricoter.com
Seattle	Weaving Works	(206)524-1221	www.weavingworks.com
Seattle	Yarn Gallery	(206)935-2010	
Sequim	Banana Belt Yarns	(360)683-5852	www.bananabeltyarns.com
Shelton	Fancy Image Yarn	(360)426-5875	www.fancyimageyarn.com
Silverdale	Linda's Knit n Stitch	(360)698-7556	
Tacoma	Lambs Ear Farm	(888)672-2288	www.lambsearfarm.com
Vancouver	Unraveled...Fine Yarns	(360)993-5835	
Vashon	Friend's Knitting	(206)567-4529	

WISCONSIN

Appleton	Jane's Knitting Hutch	(920)954-9001	www.angelfire.com/biz2/yarnshop
Delavan	Needles 'n Pins Yarn Shoppe	(608)883-9922	
Eau Claire	Yellow Dog Knitting	(715)839-7272	
Fond du Lac	Knitting Room	(920)906-4800	
Green Bay	Monterey Yarn	9208845258	
Madison	Knitting Tree	(608)238-0121	www.knittingtree.com
Madison	Lakeside Fibers	(608)257-2999	www.lakesidefibers.com
Milwaukee	Ruhama's Yarn & Fabrics	(414)332-2660	
Neenah	Yarns By Design	(888)559-2767	www.yarnsbydesign.com
Sister Bay	Easy Stitchin Needle Art	(920)854-2840	
St. Germain	Sutter's Gold 'n Fleece	(715)479-7634	www.suttersgoldnfleece.com
Stevens Point	Herrschners	(800)441-0838	www.herrschners.com
Verona	Sow's Ear	(608)848-2755	

WEST VIRGINIA

Morgantown	Needlecraft Barn	(304)296-3789	